Bird Feeders

by Ed Baldwin

COPYRIGHT © 1996
CREATIVE HOMEOWNER PRESS®
A Division of Federal Marketing Corp.
24 Park Way
Upper Saddle River, NJ 07458

Manufactured in the United States of America

Author: Ed Baldwin
Editorial Director: David Schiff
Senior Editor: Timothy O. Bakke
Assistant Editor: Patrick Quinn
Copy Editor: Beth Kalet

Art Director: Annie Jeon
Graphic Designer: Michelle D. Halko
Photographs: Scott Star Photography
Illustrator: Frank Rohrbach

Cover Design: Annie Jeon
Cover Photograph: Freeze Frame Studio

Electronic Prepress: TBC Color Imaging, Inc.
Printed at: Webcrafter Inc.

Current Printing (last digit)
10 9 8 7 6 5 4 3 2 1

Bird Feeders
Library of Congress Catalog Card Number: 94-69654
ISBN: 1-880029-46-4

Safety First

Though all the designs and methods in this book have been tested for safety, it is not possible to overstate the importance of using the safest construction methods possible. What follows are reminders; some do's and don'ts of basic carpentry. They are not substitutes for your own common sense.

- *Always* use caution, care, and good judgment when following the procedures described in this book.

- *Always* be sure that the electrical setup is safe; be sure that no circuit is overloaded, and that all power tools and electrical outlets are properly grounded. Do not use power tools in wet locations.

- *Always* read container labels on paints, solvents, and other products; provide ventilation, and observe all other warnings.

- *Always* read the tool manufacturer's instructions for using a tool, especially the warnings.

- *Always* use holders or pushers to workpieces shorter than 3 inches on a table saw or jointer. Avoid working short pieces if you can.

- *Always* remove the key from any drill chuck (portable or press) before starting the drill.

- *Always* pay deliberate attention to how a tool works so that you can avoid being injured.

- *Always* know the limitations of your tools. Do not try to force them to do what they were not designed to do.

- *Always* make sure that any adjustment is locked before proceeding. For example, always check the rip fence on a table saw or the bevel adjustment on a portable saw before starting to work.

- *Always* clamp small pieces firmly to a bench or other work surfaces when sawing or drilling.

- *Always* wear the appropriate rubber or work gloves when handling chemicals, doing heavy construction, or sanding.

- *Always* wear a disposable mask when working around odors, dust, or mist. Use a special respirator when working with toxic substances.

- *Always* wear eye protection, especially when using power tools or striking metal on metal or concrete; a chip can fly off, for example, when chiseling concrete.

- *Always* be aware that there is rarely enough time for your body's reflexes to save you from injury from a power tool in a dangerous situation; everything happens too fast. Be alert!

- *Always* keep your hands away from the business ends of blades, cutters, and bits.

- *Always* hold a portable circular saw with both hands so that you will know where your hands are.

- *Always* use a drill with an auxiliary handle to control the torque when large-size bits are used.

- *Always* check your local building codes when planning new construction. The codes are intended to protect public safety and should be observed to the letter.

- *Never* work with power tools when you are tired or under the influence of alcohol or drugs.

- *Never* cut very small pieces of wood or pipe. Whenever possible, cut small pieces off larger pieces.

- *Never* change a blade or a bit unless the power cord is unplugged. Do not depend on the switch being off; you might accidentally hit it.

- *Never* work in insufficient lighting.

- *Never* work while wearing loose clothing, hanging hair, open cuffs, or jewelry.

- *Never* work with dull tools. Have them sharpened, or learn how to sharpen them yourself.

- *Never* use a power tool on a workpiece that is not firmly supported or clamped.

- *Never* saw a workpiece that spans a large distance between horses without close support on either side of the kerf; the piece can bend, closing the kerf and jamming the blade, causing saw kickback.

- *Never* support a workpiece with your leg or other part of your body when sawing.

- *Never* carry sharp or pointed tools, such as utility knives, awls, or chisels, in your pocket. If you want to carry tools, use a special-purpose tool belt with leather pockets and holders.

Table of Contents

Introduction 6

Swiss Chalet 14

Hanging Apples 19

Suet Holder 24

Watering Hole...28

Bird~Feedosaurus 31

Color Photograph Section.........................33

Seed, Suet, and Water Station 41

Milk~Jug Seed Depot..................................46

Chickadee Feeder 48

Cozy Cottage 51

Feline Feeding Stand 54

Seed and Suet Storehouse 58

Bird Feeder/Robin's Roost 63

Tin~Can Seed Shoppe.................................68

Multilevel Seed Silo....................................71

Squirrel Feeder 74

Seed Bell Shelter...78

Pig Bird Feeder 82

Thistle Seed Dispenser................................87

Gazebo Rest Stop.......................................91

Glossary...102

Index 103

Metric Conversion Charts 104

Introduction

Among the most common of back-yard birds, and frequent visitors to bird feeders, Chickadees have a black cap and throat, white cheeks, a gray back, and light underparts. Chickadees range across much of the United States, except the extreme south. The birds often feed upside down, clinging to the underside of twigs and branches in search of insect eggs and larvae.

The brilliant red male Northern Cardinal is arguably the favorite backyard bird in the eastern United States, which comprises its year-round territory. Similar in color to the Summer Tanager, the only other all-red bird, the male Cardinal may be identified by its head crest and black face mask. The female is reddish brown with a bright red beak. Especially fond of sunflower seeds and chopped nuts, Cardinals will be daily visitors to well stocked feeders in the winter, and you should continue to spot them in the spring and summer as they nest and raise a family, though they may make less frequent trips to the feeder. Cardinals are related to grosbeaks, finches, and sparrows.

Bird-Feeding Basics

Why Feed Birds?

Perhaps you're a serious bird watcher who keeps records and identifies species. Or maybe you simply enjoy the sight and music of the graceful flying creatures. Either way, the experience is more convenient if you invite the birds to your place rather than search for them. There's no better way to attract birds to your home than by offering food. Building a bird feeder is your way of extending your hand, introducing yourself, and welcoming the birds to your home. As with any project, before you dive in there are a few basics to learn and keep in mind. Being prepared will make the process go smoothly and your relationship with nature that much better.

Birds and You

Like other living creatures, birds have basic needs: Food, water, air, and shelter. Many birds are curious creatures and will fly to any yard to help meet these needs, whether there's a feeder or not. But some birds may be leery. A bird feeder is a great way to lure reluctant birds to the yard while keeping the inquisitive ones coming back.

To get a better understanding of how to make your yard more inviting to birds, try looking at it from a bird's perspective. Take a walk around the yard. Think about what would attract a bird—and about what would keep one away. Are there any bushes or trees that produce berries or other kinds of fruit that might make your home more attractive, as compared with your neighbors' homes or the park down the street? If so, you can keep the birds coming back with a feeder after the berries are gone. If not, you'll lure birds with fruit and seed laid out on a bird feeder.

Is there anywhere for a thirsty traveling bird to get a drink or wash its weary wings? Look up, and you may notice that nook in the tree that catches water after a rainstorm. But even natural basins like that may go dry quickly, which is why birds are sometimes hard pressed to find valuable water. Putting out a shallow water trough will make your yard more alluring.

Look at the thick bush that would be a great place to build a nest and start a family. From a bird's perspective, that bush is also a great place for a predator to hide. The cat that cuddles on your lap, purring so innocently, for example, won't treat birds with the same affection. Keep this kind of bird-safety consideration in mind when you plan where to locate a bird feeder in your yard.

Where to Place Your Feeder

When you survey your yard, be aware of areas that are in the open and those that are close to trees and bushes or your house. Few birds like to eat in open areas where they're exposed and most vulnerable to predators. Sometimes even another bird, such as a hawk, can be an enemy in open areas. An ideal environment for a bird consists of a mixture of trees, shrubs, flowers, grasses, and climbing vines. Not every home can offer all these settings, of course. But even one or two will usually be enough.

You may have to try a few spots in the yard before you find the best one for your feeder. You might notice that one location gives the squirrels easy access to the feeder, so you end up feeding more squirrels than birds. If the feeder is within 8 feet of a tree limb or trunk, for example, a squirrel will be able to jump onto the feeder easily, no matter what precautions you take. Another spot may be too far out in the open and doesn't attract as many birds as you would like. You may place the feeder in another place only to discover that the birds don't come, and you have no idea why.

A good point to remember is that many birds, such as chickadees, titmice, and nuthatches, like to get a mouthful of food, then return to a tree or bush. Try to keep their bird feeders close to quick cover, but not so close that predators will be able to hide and sneak up on the birds. The cover should be a tree or high bush at least 5 or 6 feet off the ground. Any ground cover should be at least 8 feet from the feeder to prevent ambush attacks from predators.

Discouraging Competitors and Predators

If you're building your feeder expecting to attract only birds, you'll probably be in for a surprise. Birds aren't the only wild animals willing to accept your offer of free food. The animals that will visit your feeder fall into two categories: competitors, who want to eat the bird's food, and predators, who want to eat the birds. In most areas the foremost competitors for bird food are squirrels, although you might find raccoons, skunks, and opossums raiding the feeder at night. The most common predator in suburban neighborhoods is the prowling house cat. In some areas you might find snakes, birds of prey, and even dogs threatening the birds at your feeder.

When it comes to keeping the food away from hungry competitors like squirrels, often people give up and let the little bandits eat the food—although they might throw in an occasional holler from the kitchen or knock on the window. But if you do choose to battle, be prepared. It's going to be a challenge to keep the squirrels and other unwanted guests away from your feeder.

Baffles and Other Techniques. To protect your bird feeders from piracy, make them hard to get at by using baffles on the lines they hang from or the posts they sit on. Squirrels will most likely be your main concern. Watch out, because these clever creatures just won't give in. They'll do almost anything—contort their bodies, jump incredible distances, take any path—to get at the food you put out for the birds. Because squirrels are so determined, often the best strategy is to supply them with their own food source. The logic here is that if you provide the little gluttons with easy access to their own well-stocked feeder, you might distract them from the less accessible bird feeders. With this idea in mind, you'll find building instructions for the Squirrel Feeder on page 74.

A good way to discourage food thieves from reaching a feeder secured to the top of a post or pole is to place aluminum sheeting on the post (the sheeting can also be wrapped around a tree). Animals such as cats and squirrels that rely on their claws to climb trees, wooden posts, or galvanized-steel poles, can't get a grip on smooth aluminum. There are a few alternatives to this technique, as shown in Bird-Feeder Baffles, page 9. You can simply wrap the aluminum flush around the post; you can make the aluminum into a cone shape, with the open end facing downward; or you can use an aluminum disc attached to a pole with a spring.

With a suspended feeder, hang baffles along the wire or chain to hinder squirrels from climbing along the suspension and reaching the feeder. Pie tins with a hole punctured in the center or clear plastic soda bottles with a hole poked through the bottom work great for this purpose.

Try enclosing the feeder area with chicken wire to prevent the animals from building up speed and jumping onto the feeder. If your feeder rests on top of a metal pole, you can grease the pole with petroleum jelly to reduce traction. You can also grease the wire from which a feeder hangs. If you have a cat, try attaching a bell to the cat's collar. The sound may alert the birds to imminent danger.

Bird Food

In addition to using up scraps of wood when you build it, a bird feeder gives you a chance to use up scraps of food. Nothing needs to be wasted. Instead of throwing out an apple core, place it in a feeder or on a skewer if your feeder has one. Cedar waxwings, finches, jays, mockingbirds, orioles, robins, and woodpeckers are known to eat apples. Don't toss out the stale bread and donuts or the bread crust that your kids—or you—don't like. Give it to the birds. You can also try leftover pasta, rice, potatoes, cheese, and fatty meats like bacon and hamburger. Experiment to see what the birds will eat, and

Downy Woodpeckers (left) and the similar-looking but larger Hairy Woodpeckers are the most likely woodpeckers to visit your bird feeder. Downies will eat any kind of food you'd normally offer in a feeder, but they're fond of sunflower seed, cracked corn, and suet, especially in the winter. The black-and-white sparrow-sized birds have a smaller beak than you might expect for a woodpecker; male Downies have a large red spot on the back of the neck. You'll find Downies throughout the U.S., except the extreme Southwest.

what they'll avoid. Keep a daily/weekly log of what you offer and which birds show up; that way you'll have it documented for future reference.

Suet, commonly made from the hard fat trimmed from the kidneys and loins of beef or lamb, is a favorite among many birds. You can make your own suet by rendering any animal fat or saving the melted fat you get when preparing dinner. Mix the fat with flour or cornmeal and table scraps, peanut butter, or seeds to create a high-energy snack for bluebirds, chickadees, creepers, crows, finches, flickers, jays, magpies, starlings, thrashers, titmice, woodpeckers, and wrens.

Of course, seeds and nuts are staples for the bird species that frequent feeders. Most grocery stores and home centers carry standard varieties of birdseed, including sunflower seeds (whole or hulled), cracked corn, and wild bird food mixes, so selecting the seed won't be a problem. Look in specialty pet stores for a more exotic selection of seed, such as buckwheat, hemp, rape, safflower, thistle (niger), and various kinds of millet seed. These seeds are often preferred by small, colorful songbirds. You can also put out almonds, filberts, raw peanuts, and walnuts, whole or chopped, for larger birds such as jays, cardinals, and woodpeckers.

Like all animals, birds need to drink water. Water containers are included in the plans for the Seed, Suet, and

Bird-Feeder Baffles

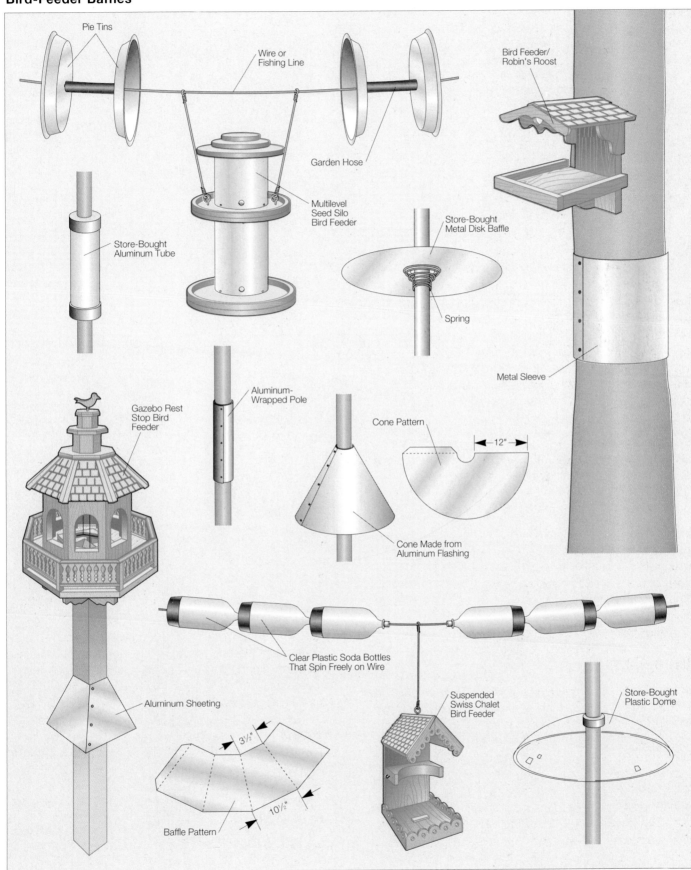

Pie Tins

Wire or Fishing Line

Garden Hose

Multilevel Seed Silo Bird Feeder

Store-Bought Aluminum Tube

Store-Bought Metal Disk Baffle

Spring

Bird Feeder/ Robin's Roost

Metal Sleeve

Gazebo Rest Stop Bird Feeder

Aluminum-Wrapped Pole

Cone Pattern

←—12"—→

Cone Made from Aluminum Flashing

Aluminum Sheeting

3½"

10½"

Baffle Pattern

Clear Plastic Soda Bottles That Spin Freely on Wire

Suspended Swiss Chalet Bird Feeder

Store-Bought Plastic Dome

Favorite Foods of Backyard Birds

Most birds eat a variety of small seeds, including cracked corn, millet, niger (thistle) seed, oats, peanuts, rape seed, safflower seed, and sunflower seed. Others prefer nuts, fruit, or suet. Below is a list of some common backyard birds and their food preferences.

	Berries/Fruit	Bread/Pasta	Cheese	Meat	Nuts	Seeds/Grain	Suet
Bluebirds	O		O		O		O
Cardinals	O	O			O	O	
Catbirds	O		O		O		O
Cedar Waxwings	O		O				
Chickadees	O	O			O	O	O
Cowbirds	O	O			O	O	
Creepers			O		O		O
Crows	O	O	O	O	O	O	O
Finches	O	O	O	O	O	O	O
Flickers	O				O		O
Grosbeaks	O					O	
Jays	O	O			O	O	O
Juncos		O			O	O	O
Magpies	O	O		O		O	O
Mockingbirds	O				O		O
Nuthatches					O	O	O
Orioles	O				O		O
Robins	O	O	O		O		O
Red-Winged Blackbirds	O	O			O	O	O
Sparrows	O	O	O	O	O	O	
Starlings	O	O	O	O	O	O	O
Tanagers	O	O			O		
Thrashers	O	O			O	O	O
Thrushes	O				O		
Titmice		O			O	O	O
Woodpeckers	O	O	O	O	O	O	O
Wrens	O	O			O		O

Daily or Weekly Log

Weekly Log							
Date	Bird Food Used	Which Feeder	Type of Birds Attracted	Predator Problems	Attempts at Stopping Predators and Results	When was Feeder Last Filled	Notes
1/12	SUET	SUET FEEDER	BLUE JAYS FLICKERS	SQUIRRELS ATE ALL THE FOOD	BAFFLE; SQUIRREL CLIMBED OVER	1/10	NO ROBINS SHOWED AGAIN

Water Station project on page 41 and the Watering Hole project on page 28. These feeders will keep the birds' thirst quenched, and keep them clean if they decide to take a bath.

CONSTRUCTING BIRD FEEDERS

Many of the bird feeders included in this collection require minimal woodworking skills to complete, and most of the techniques used are simple and straightforward. You'll need only simple hand tools for a number of the projects, and except for one, the Gazebo Rest Stop, the most advanced tools you'll need are a table saw and a router, although a band saw will come in handy for some jobs. The Gazebo project requires a band saw or scroll saw to complete the project as shown.

Because your bird feeder will be outside, you'll want to build it of durable, weather-resistant materials. Here's a look at the materials to use:

Wood. Redwood, cypress, white cedar, and western red cedar are often used for outdoor projects because they are naturally rot resistant. They are also attractive and easy to work with. Other softwoods, such as Douglas fir, hemlock, pine, and spruce, rot more quickly. If you hang your bird feeder in a sunny spot, however, it will dry out before rot can take hold, especially if you paint it. Exterior grade plywood is also a good choice if you paint it well and seal any exposed edges.

Wood that has been pressure-treated with chromated copper arsenic (CCA) is extremely rot resistant, but the Environmental Protection Agency does not recommend its use for applications that will be in contact with animal feed. If you use pressure-treated wood in your project, reserve it for support posts and brackets (parts with which the birds won't come in contact). Also, bear in mind that the dust created when you saw or sand pressure-treated lumber is toxic, so wear a dust mask when you work with it. If children are participating in the building project, you may not want to use pressure-treated wood.

Fasteners. Select hardware and fasteners that are resistant to rust. Galvanized bugle head screws, often sold as "deck screws," are economical and easy to use. Likewise, galvanized nails retard rust. Stainless steel nails hold up well outdoors, but they're expensive. Brass screws also won't rust and can be attractive, but they break easily and the heads strip out easily, so be sure to predrill. Another way to thwart rust and give your project a finished look is to countersink the screws and nails, then fill the holes with wood plugs or wood filler.

Adhesives. There are several adhesive products that are rated for exterior use. The bird feeders in this book are

Fasteners

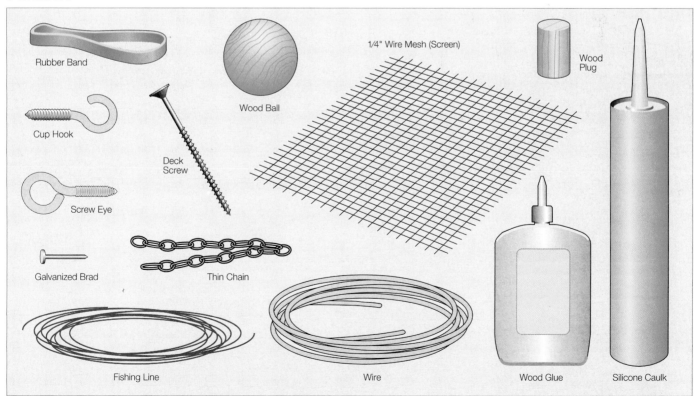

Rubber Band

Cup Hook

Screw Eye

Galvanized Brad

Deck Screw

Thin Chain

Wood Ball

1/4" Wire Mesh (Screen)

Wood Plug

Fishing Line

Wire

Wood Glue

Silicone Caulk

Tools

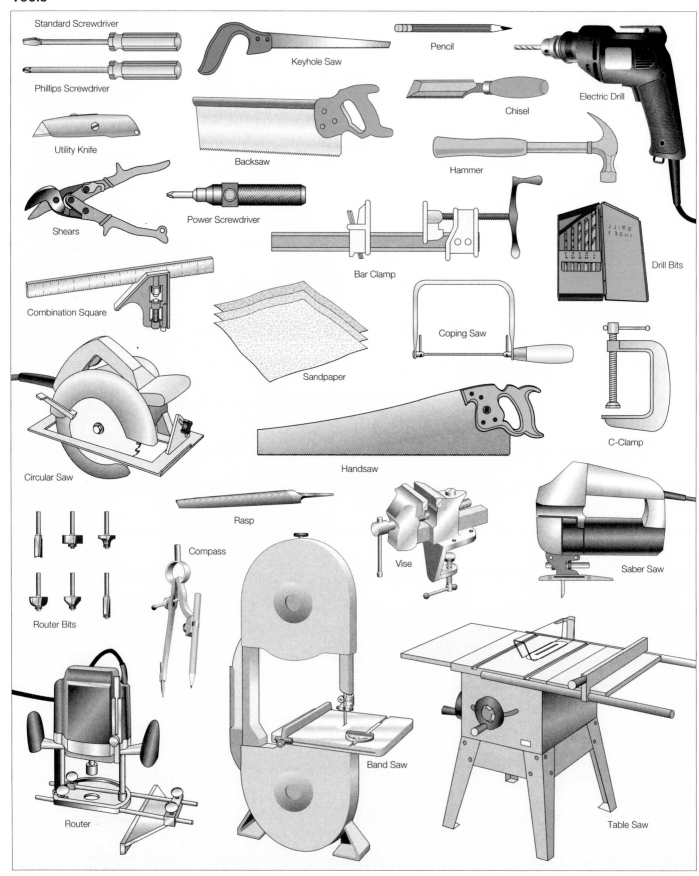

Standard Screwdriver

Phillips Screwdriver

Utility Knife

Shears

Combination Square

Circular Saw

Router Bits

Router

Keyhole Saw

Backsaw

Power Screwdriver

Bar Clamp

Sandpaper

Handsaw

Rasp

Compass

Band Saw

Pencil

Chisel

Hammer

Coping Saw

Vise

Electric Drill

Drill Bits

C-Clamp

Saber Saw

Table Saw

assembled with clear silicone caulk, along with exterior-quality wood glue in some places. Silicone holds and yet is flexible enough to yield when the wood swells in a rain or shrinks in the sun. Several acrylic-based silicone substitutes can also be used, but since acrylic is a water-based product some warping of the wood may occur.

Finishes. Exterior paint is the most effective way to preserve outdoor wood. Many of the projects shown in this book have been embellished with decorative painting. This is intended to give you some painting ideas. If you don't have the inclination or skill for such work, don't worry, most of the projects will look fine with simple paint jobs or no paint at all.

American Goldfinches are best known for the canary yellow and black cap and wings of the male in the spring and summer. Females—and males in the fall and winter—are gray-brown with yellow highlights and black wings. You'll attract American Gold-finches, which appear throughout the U.S. at one time or another during the year, if you offer thistle seed, their favorite food.

For a natural look, give your project a few coats of wood sealer/preservative (the same stuff that is sold for maintaining outdoor decks). You can also use a semitransparent or solid house-siding stain. And of course, no finish at all is often a fine choice. A feeder built of rot-resistant wood hung in a sunny spot will last for years, while weathering to a pleasing gray.

FINAL CONSIDERATIONS

Birds attract other birds. The more feeders you have, the more likely you will attract a greater variety of birds. And in cold weather, nonmigrating birds benefit from the ready food source you'll hand out in the feeders. It's important to note that once you start feeding birds you're making a commitment. It's cruel and irresponsible to start feeding birds, especially in winter, and then remove the only food source they have come to recognize.

Take a look around your neighborhood and see who else has a bird feeder. This may be one of the best ways to learn good local tips. Find out what has worked for others and what hasn't worked. Maybe there's a club in your neighborhood that involves bird watching or feeding birds. If there isn't, you might like to start one.

Feeding birds can be rewarding in several ways. You can feel good about helping the little creatures, especially during winter when naturally occurring food sources are scarce. You can also have fun watching the antics of the acrobatic flying animals as they compete for free seed.

Speaking of fun, most people with any kind of mechanical ability derive satisfaction from making something with their hands. To that end, the projects range from basic to ornate so everyone can enjoy themselves in the shop. And although all the feeders are practical feeding stations, some are deliberately whimsical in design to maximize the fun.

Related to the Black-Capped Chickadee, the Tufted Titmouse is gray, with beige-and-rust-colored lower parts. The bird shows its predominant feature, the head crest, to show it's feeling aggressive or threatened, as when it's competing for food. Titmice are abundant in the eastern half of the U.S.; you can attract them with sunflower seeds and suet.

Swiss Chalet

Decorative trim work, fancy wood shingles, and a steep roof that protects both birds and birdseed give this feeder an Old World look.

D on't throw out the juice jar when it's empty; you can use it to make this feeder. You can also use scrap wood for some of the parts, so take a look around your basement before you buy anything.

The Swiss Chalet feeder is easy to refill and clean—just remove the rubber band and take out the jar. The roof protects the seed from rain and snow. You might want to use a band saw to make the decorative trim and wood shin-

gles, but these parts are optional. You can simplify the project by stopping at Step 4.

All in all, the feeder is a great weekend project. See whether your chalet will lure a blackbird or flicker away from the insects to munch on birdseed. A good point to keep in mind, since the jar holds a lot of seed, is that it costs less to buy a large quantity of birdseed all at once than it does to buy many small bags.

CUTTING & MATERIALS LIST

Part	Quantity	Dimensions	Part	Quantity	Dimensions
Base	1	¾"x7¼"x7¼"	Ridge trim	2	⅛"x½"x7½"
Back	1	¾"x7¼"x14"	Cup hooks	2	½" diameter
Long roof piece	1	¾"x7¼"x7¾"	Deck screws		1⅝" long
Short roof piece	1	¾"x7¼"x7"	Brads		¾" long
Jar holder	1	1½"x3"x7¼"	Juice jar	1	Quart size
Jar support	1	¼"x½"x3"	Silicone caulk		
Front base trim	1	¼"x1½"x7¾"	Screw eyes	2	¾" diameter
Side base trim	2	¼"x1½"x7½"	Paint or stain		
Shingles	18	⅛"x2¼"x9¼"			

Difficulty Level:

Overall View

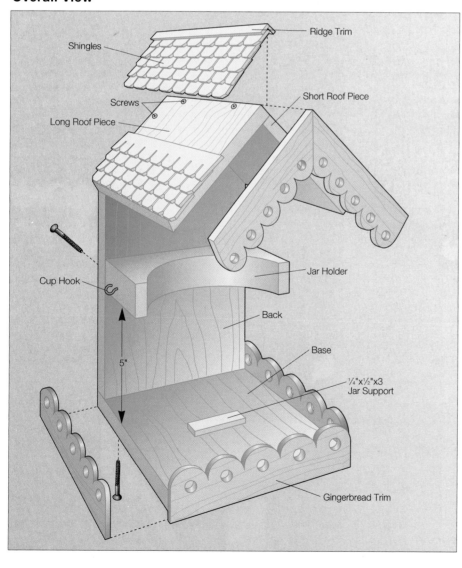

Ridge Trim

Shingles

Screws

Short Roof Piece

Long Roof Piece

Cup Hook

Jar Holder

5"

Back

Base

¼"x½"x3"
Jar Support

Gingerbread Trim

BUILDING THE FEEDER

1 Cut and Assemble the Frame. Cut the base, back, and roof pieces to the dimensions in the Cutting List. Standard 1x8 boards are actually 7¼ inches wide, so you'll only need to crosscut the pieces to length. Use a protractor or combination square to lay out the 45-degree cuts at the top of the back as shown in Back-Piece Layout, then cut the angles.

Lap the long roof board over the short one and secure them with two screws. Place the roof assembly over the back piece and use four screws and glue to attach them as shown in the Overall View. Next, attach the base to the back by driving three screws up from underneath.

2 Attach the Jar Holder and Support. The jar holder has a curve cut into it to fit the jar. Use the jar you've selected to lay out the curve so that it goes about halfway into the 3-inch depth of the holder. Cut the curve with a coping saw or saber saw. Position the holder

Back-Piece Layout

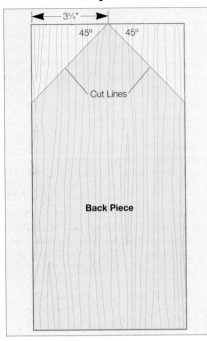

Back Piece

5 inches up from the base and attach it with glue and two screws driven through the back piece. Attach a cup hook to each side of the jar holder.

The jar support is a small piece of wood or plywood that lifts the jar slightly from the base to allow a controlled amount of seed to spill out. Cut the support to the size in the Cutting List and attach it to the base with one brad.

Set the jar on the support piece and rest it against the curved holder. Place a rubber band around the jar and loop the ends around the holder's cup hooks to hold the jar in position.

3 Make and Attach the Gingerbread Trim. All five pieces of gingerbread trim are sliced off one 8¼-inch-long piece of two-by stock ripped to 3 inches. Although technically you only need a 1¾-inch-wide piece to make the five slices and allow for saw-kerf waste, it's better to use a wider piece so you won't have to get your hands too close to the saw blade.

First, use a compass to lay out 1½-inch-diameter semicircles along the length of the piece. Then drill ½-inch-diameter holes through the entire piece, centering the holes on the marks made by the compass points as shown in Drilling Holes in the Gingerbread Trim. Cut the semicircles along the length of the

Drilling Holes in the Gingerbread Trim

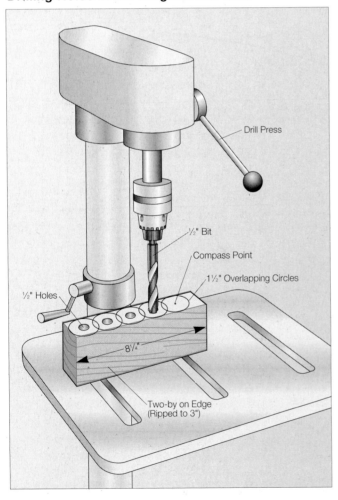

Cutting the Semicircles

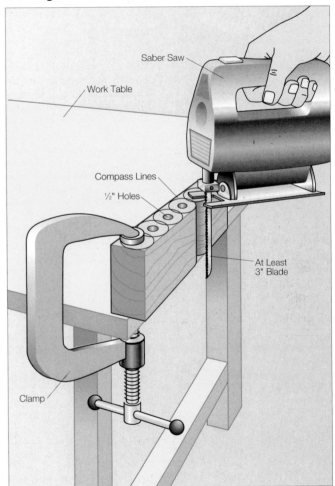

Slicing the Gingerbread Trim

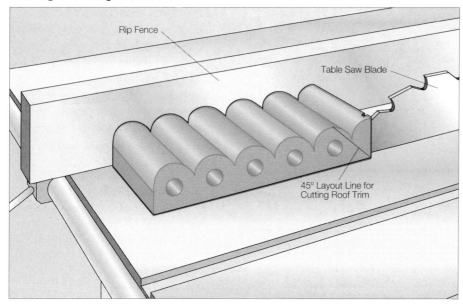

Rip Fence

Table Saw Blade

45° Layout Line for
Cutting Roof Trim

Make 45-degree-angle cuts at one
end of the roof-trim pieces. (Note
that the roof trim is ½ inch longer
than the roof.) Attach the roof trim
with glue and brads. Cut the base
trim to length and attach it with glue
and brads. If you plan to paint the
feeder, you may want to do it now,
so you don't have to worry about
getting paint on the roof.

4 **Make the Shingles and
Ridge Trim.** For the shingles,
cut five 2¼-inch-wide pieces off a
length of 2x10 as shown in Cutting
the Shingle Blocks. You'll get about
four shingle courses from each of
the five pieces. Cut 1-inch-deep
kerfs spaced about 1 inch apart.
Use a band saw, or run the piece
through a table saw with the blade
set 1 inch high as shown in Kerfing
the Shingle Blocks.

piece with a band saw or saber saw
as shown in Cutting the Semicircles.
Use the band saw or a table saw to
rip five ¼x1½-inch slices from the
block. If you use a table saw, reset

the fence for each cut so you can
keep the thin piece on the outside of
the blade, not between the blade
and the fence, as shown in Slicing
the Gingerbread Trim.

Make 45-degree cuts with a band
saw or coping saw about ¼ inch up

Cutting the Shingle Blocks

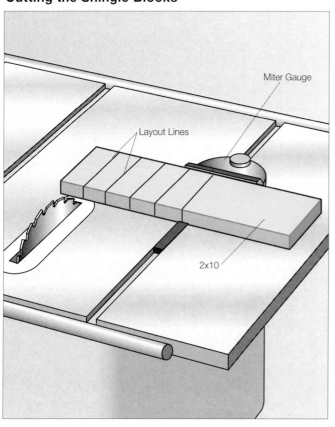

Miter Gauge

Layout Lines

2x10

Kerfing the Shingle Blocks

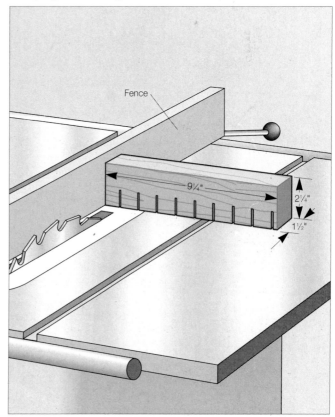

Fence

9¼"

2¼"

1½"

Beveling the Shingles

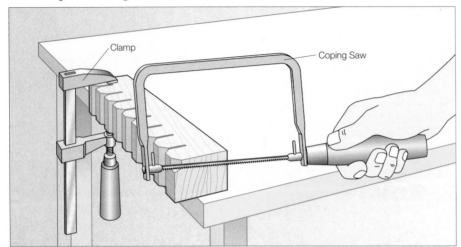

Clamp

Coping Saw

Slicing the Shingles

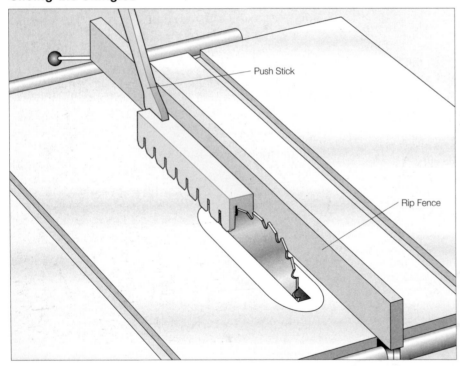

Push Stick

Rip Fence

on each kerf as shown in Beveling the Shingles to give a Victorian look to the shingles. You can slice the shingles from the board with a band saw, but because the shingles are only ⅛ inch thick you might find it easier to do on the table saw as shown in Slicing the Shingles. Slice one extra piece and rip the full side to ½-inch-wide pieces to use for the ridge trim.

5 **Shingle the Roof.** Set the shingles using only silicone sealant. Let the first course of shingles overhang the eaves by about ½ inch. As you work your way up the roof, overlap the shingles by about half their length and slip them to the right or left so that the saw kerfs don't line up in successive courses.

Add the ½-inch-wide trim pieces to the ridge. When the adhesive sets, use a coping saw to trim the shingles flush to the back of the feeder; they should overhang the front of the feeder by about ¼ inch. Be careful and cut slowly; the shingles are fragile.

Attach screw eyes to the ridge in front and back and hang the feeder from a tree branch or roof overhang.

Hanging Apples

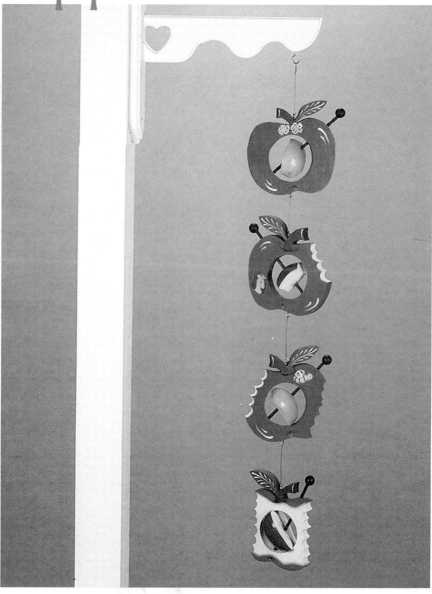

An apple a day may keep the doctor away, but these apples will keep birds coming to your yard for years to come. This feeder holds bulk foods and is easily made from scrap wood.

Chomp! Chomp! Chomp! Chomp! This whimsical bird feeder depicts an apple in four stages of consumption. You should be able to finish the hanging feeder in an afternoon with a few hand tools and some pieces of scrap wood. Bird-feeder projects like this are a great way to start kids off at woodworking, as long as you supervise them.

This kind of feeder is designed to hold bulk food, not birdseed. Small wooden skewers hold the food in place. Suet is the most energy-efficient food for insect-eating birds in the winter; in the summer, try hanging out a piece of stale muffin or biscuit, or even a slice of fruit, as a dietary supplement. Expect starlings to take over and bully other birds when you put out suet; it's one of their favorites. Any scraps of food that fall to the ground will be picked up by ground-feeding birds such as cardinals, jays, sparrows, doves, and chickadees.

The instructions assume that you'll build all four stages of the apple-shaped feeder. You can scale down the project accordingly if you're interested in only a section or two. This feeder works well with the Bird-Feeder Hanger on page 22.

CUTTING & MATERIALS LIST

Part	Quantity	Dimensions	Part	Quantity	Dimensions
Apple shape	4	¾"x6½"x6¾"	Cup hook	1	⅝" diameter
Wood skewers	4	¼" diameter x7"	Glue		
Wood balls	4	¾" diameter	Paint		
Screw eyes	7	⅜" diameter	Wire or fishing line		

Difficulty Level:

BUILDING THE FEEDER

1 Transfer the Pattern. Each of the four apples has the same shape, except for the bites taken out of them. Begin by transferring the pattern for the apple shape onto four pieces of 1x8 lumber. The pattern shown is 50 percent of its actual size. To make it full-size, reproduce it on a photocopier set at 200 percent. Or you can use the grid to make patterns of any size you want. Of course, you don't have to copy the pattern precisely. You can sketch your own apple designs if you like. Cut the pattern out and use tape or contact adhesive to place it directly onto your stock. If you plan to make multiple copies of the feeder, glue the pattern to thicker paperboard. Cut out the paperboard pattern, then outline the pattern onto the pieces of wood.

2 Cut Out the Apples. For each apple, drill a starter hole and cut the center opening before you start cutting the outer shapes. Use a coping saw or saber saw. To use a coping saw, disassemble the blade, thread it through the starter hole, and reassemble the blade.

After cutting out the center, cut the successive bites from your pattern and trace the bites onto the apples. Or if you like, you can create your own bites. Now cut out the apples, with the bites taken out, using a

Apple Cutout Pattern

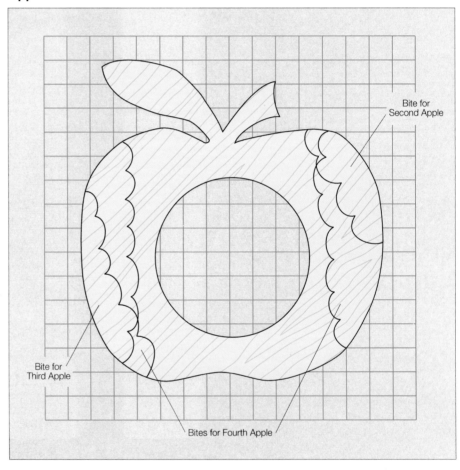

Bite for Second Apple

Bite for Third Apple

Bites for Fourth Apple

coping saw or saber saw. When cutting out the bites, be careful not to split the apple along the grain. Sand the cut pieces, removing all rough edges.

3 Drill the Skewer Holes. Mount the apple pieces in a wood vise or sandwich them with clamps or an all-purpose vise between two scrap pieces of wood.

Using a ¼-inch bit, drill a hole at an angle as shown for the skewer. Drill only through the top section of the apple. Take your time, and be certain that you center the bit and keep it straight as you drill. The exact angle of skewers isn't important, but notice that in all but the last piece the skewer enters the apple near the leaf. In the last piece the skewer enters the apple near the stem.

Attaching and Hanging Cutouts

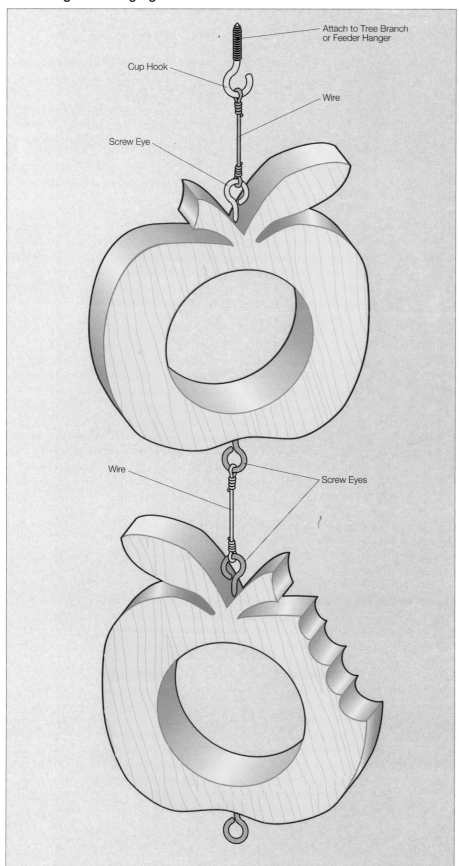

Attach to Tree Branch or Feeder Hanger

Cup Hook

Wire

Screw Eye

Wire

Screw Eyes

4 Make the Skewers. Measure and cut the ¼-inch wood dowels 7 inches long. Sharpen one end like a pencil. Stick the skewer through the hole that was drilled in Step 3 and mark where it meets the inner part of the apple. Notch out a hole for the end of the skewer with a fine chisel. If you have a ¼-inch drill bit that's at least 6 inches long, you can drill a hole for the end of the skewer. The hole needs to be only about ¼ inch deep.

The wood balls are available at most hobby stores and home centers. Secure the balls in a vise, or clamp them between scraps of wood and drill ¼-inch holes ⅜ inch deep. Another way to hold the balls is to drill a ¾-inch hole in a piece of scrap wood, put the balls in the hole, and tape them in place. Then drill through the tape. After you've prepared the balls, glue them to the ends of the wood dowels.

5 Finish the Feeder. Paint the outsides of the apples red, the leaves green, the stems brown, and the skewers black.

Attach a screw eye to the top of each apple shape, and to the bottom of each one but the last. Hang the apples in succession using wire or fishing line, allowing about a 3-inch space between them. You can hang the feeder from a tree using the cup hook, or use the Bird-Feeder Hanger on page 22 to attach it to a tree trunk, tall fence post, or the side of your house.

NOTE: *Over time, juice from the fruit may expand the skewer, making it difficult to insert the skewer back into the feeder. If this expansion happens, sand the skewer down until it fits snugly.*

CUTTING & MATERIALS LIST (FOR FEEDER HANGER)

Part	Quantity	Dimensions	Part	Quantity	Dimensions
Vertical board	1	¾"x2¼"x14", cut to shape	Deck screws (or 12d nails)	2	3" long
Horizontal board	1	¾"x3¼"x13½", cut to shape	Cup hook	1	⅝" diameter
Deck screws	2	1½" long	Glue		

Difficulty Level:

BUILDING A BIRD-FEEDER HANGER

If you don't have a tree branch where you can hang your feeder and get a good view of the birds, you can build a hanger. Position the hanger so you can easily get to the feeder for periodic cleaning and fill-ups.

1 **Trace the Pattern.** Transfer the board patterns onto pieces of 1x4 or ¾-inch plywood. The patterns shown are 50 percent of their actual size. To make them full-size, reproduce them on a photocopier set at 200 percent. You can also use the grid to make patterns of any size you want. Cut the patterns out and use tape or contact adhesive to place them directly onto your stock. If you

plan to make multiple hangers, glue the patterns to thicker paperboard. Cut out the paperboard patterns, then outline the patterns onto the pieces of wood. Cut out the shapes using a coping saw or saber saw. You can make long straight cuts on a table saw. Drill a starter hole in the horizontal board before you begin cutting out the heart. Round-over the top edge of the horizontal piece with

Feeder Hanger Pattern

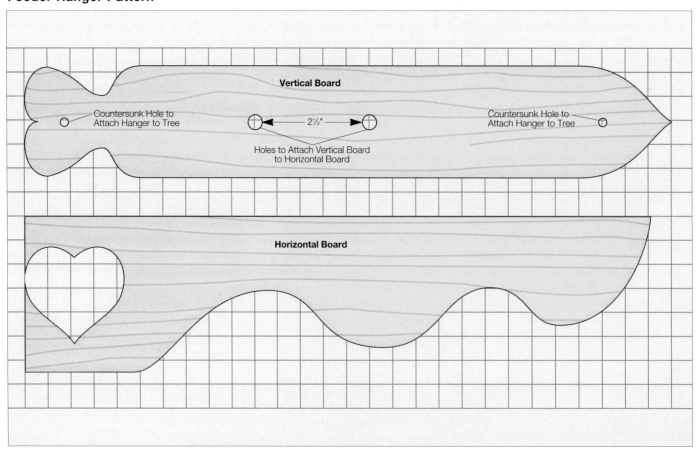

Vertical Board

Countersunk Hole to Attach Hanger to Tree

2½"

Holes to Attach Vertical Board to Horizontal Board

Countersunk Hole to Attach Hanger to Tree

Horizontal Board

a rasp, 80-grit sandpaper, or a router equipped with a ¼-inch roundover bit. You can round the other edges of both pieces or rout them with a ¼-inch roundover bit set ⅛ inch deep into the surface.

2 **Assemble and Attach the Hanger.** Drill and countersink two holes in the top and bottom of the vertical board, as shown in Feeder Hanger. These holes will be used to mount the hanger assembly.

Drill two centered, countersunk holes in the back of the vertical board, 2½ inches apart as shown in the drawing. Connect the vertical and horizontal boards using glue and two 1½-inch screws driven through the back of the vertical board into the horizontal one.

Screw a cup hook to the horizontal board as shown in the drawing to hold the feeder. Fasten the hanger to a tree, a post, or the side of your house using 3-inch-long screws or 12d nails.

Feeder Hanger

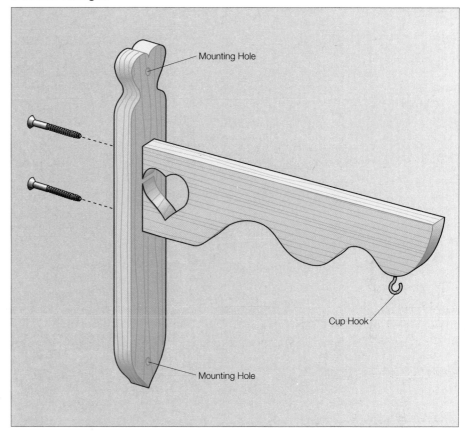

Mounting Hole

Cup Hook

Mounting Hole

Suet Holder

High-energy suet is the food of choice for insect-eating birds during winter, and this design makes it easy to dispense. During the summer, fill the feeder with bread because suet will spoil.

Did you know that some birds must consume twice their weight in food every day just to survive? Obviously, meeting the minimum daily requirement can be quite a challenge, especially in the winter when food isn't readily available.

Because of its high calorie content, suet can be an important supplement for our flying friends. A fat/seed mixture makes survival that much easier, particularly for insect-eating birds.

The suet holder is simple to fill because it's designed with a little door that flips open. But remember to keep an eye on the feeder and keep it filled. Birds will come to depend on the food you supply and may change their foraging habits accordingly. Consistent feeding may also attract some new and unusual birds looking for a good place to eat. Put bread in the feeder during warm months when suet can spoil.

CUTTING & MATERIALS LIST

Part	Quantity	Dimensions	Part	Quantity	Dimensions
Hanger	1	¾"x2½"x14"	Narrow ridge trim	1	¼"x½"x6"
Back	1	¾"x5½"x10¾"	Wood dowels	2	⁵⁄₁₆" diameter x2½" long
Long roof piece	1	¾"x5½"x6¼"			
Short roof piece	1	¾"x5½"x5½"	Hinge		½"x3"
Feed-chamber sides	2	¾"x2½"x5¼"	¼" Wire mesh		7"x6"
Feed-chamber bottom	1	¾"x2½"x7"	Deck screws		1⅝" long
Chamber side trim	2	¼"x¾"x6"	Deck screws		1¼" long
Chamber bottom trim	2	¼"x¾"x7"	Brads		¾" long
Gable trim	1	¼" thick, cut to shape	Glue		
Shingles	10	⅛"x2½"x6"	Silicone sealant		
Wide ridge trim	1	¼"x¾"x6"	Paint or stain		

Difficulty Level:

BUILDING THE FEEDER

1 **Make the Frame.** Cut the back and the long and short roof pieces to the dimensions in the Cutting List. Lap the long roof section over the short section with two countersunk 1⅝-inch screws.

Use a protractor or a combination square to lay out the 45-degree cuts at the top of the back. Cut the roof slopes, then use two 1⅝-inch screws to attach the roof assembly on top of the back piece.

2 **Assemble and Attach the Feed Chamber.** Cut the feed-chamber sides and bottom to the dimensions in the Cutting List. Fasten the bottom of the feed chamber to the sides using two 1⅝-inch screws driven up through the bottom and into each side.

The feed-chamber trim is made of ¼x¾-inch screen molding, which you can purchase at any lumberyard or home center. Cut the chamber side and bottom trim to the dimen-

Overall View

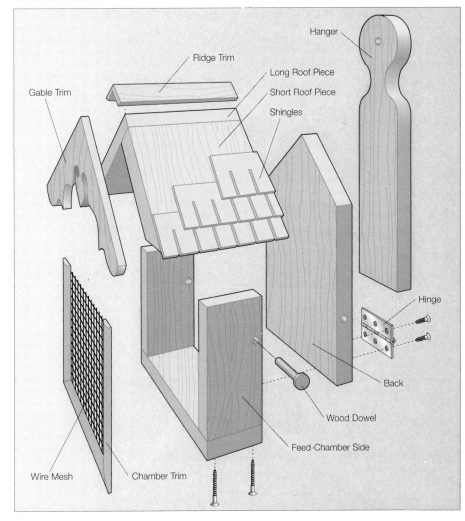

Ridge Trim
Gable Trim
Long Roof Piece
Short Roof Piece
Shingles
Hanger
Hinge
Back
Wood Dowel
Feed-Chamber Side
Wire Mesh
Chamber Trim

sions in the Cutting List. Miter-cut both ends of the bottom trim and one end of each side trim piece. Sandwich the wire mesh between the chamber and the trim, and secure the trim and mesh with brads.

Attach the feed chamber to the back piece using a hinge and the screws supplied with it. Place the hinge from behind. To make the two dowel "key" openings, drill two $5/16$-inch holes $1\frac{1}{2}$ inches down from the top edge of the feed-chamber sides. Make the holes 2 inches deep, through the sides of the feed chamber and into the sides of the back piece. (See the Feline Feeding Stand, page 54 on how to use a piece of tape on your drill bit as a depth guide.) Insert wood dowels to hold the chamber in place.

3 Make and Attach the Hanger and Gable Trim.

Enlarge the Hanger and Gable Trim Patterns by reproducing them on a photocopy machine set at 200 percent. If you don't have access to an enlarging photocopier, you can use the grid to make your own patterns. Cut out the patterns. Tape the hanger pattern to a piece of one-by stock and the gable trim pattern to a piece of $\frac{1}{2}$-inch-thick plywood. Cut around the patterns with a coping saw or saber saw. Round-over the edges of the upper three-quarters of the hanger with a $\frac{1}{4}$-inch roundover bit in a router or with a rasp and sandpaper. Drill a hole in the top center of the hanger as shown.

Center the hanger in the middle of the back piece, 4 inches up from the bottom of the feeder. Secure the hanger in place with glue and two $1\frac{1}{4}$-inch screws driven through the hanger and into the back of the feeder.

Fasten the trim to the front edge of the roof with glue and brads. Sink the nails with a nail set and fill the dimples with wood putty.

4 Shingle and Trim the Roof.

First, cut three $2\frac{1}{2}$-inch-wide pieces off a length of 2x8 as shown in Cutting the Shingle Blocks. Then cut 1-inch-deep kerfs spaced about 1 inch apart, using a band saw or a table saw as shown in Kerfing the Shingle Blocks. Slice the shingles $\frac{1}{8}$ inch thick with the band saw or table saw as shown in Slicing the Shingles. You'll get about four shingle courses from each of the three pieces. Cut the shingles to fit the roof with a $\frac{1}{4}$-inch overhang at the rake ends and flush in the back where you attach the hanger. Let the shingles overhang the eaves by about $\frac{1}{2}$ inch. Secure the shingles to the roof with dabs of silicone,

Hanger and Gable Trim Patterns

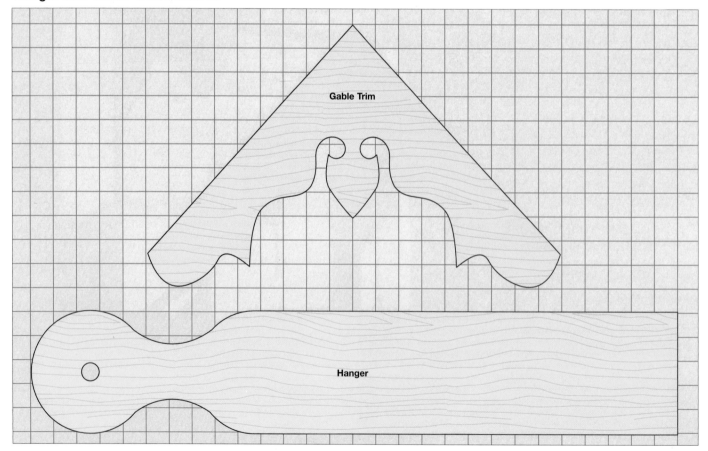

Gable Trim

Hanger

overlapping them by about 1 inch as you move up the roof.

Cut the ridge trim to the dimensions in the Cutting List. Attach the trim to the roof, lapping the wide section over the narrow section, with silicone and brads.

5 **Finish the Feeder.** Paint or stain the project the color(s) of your choice. Fill the feeder with suet or bread and hang it in your back-yard on a pole or tree. Be sure to press the food against the wire mesh so the birds can get at it easily.

Cutting the Shingle Blocks

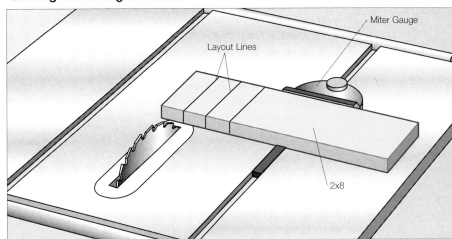

Kerfing the Shingle Blocks

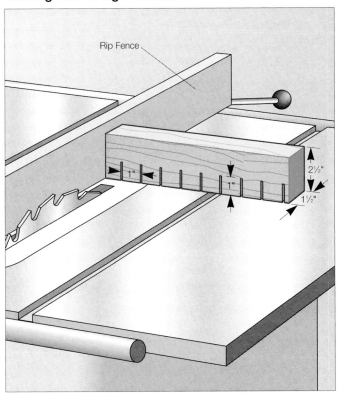

Slicing the Shingles

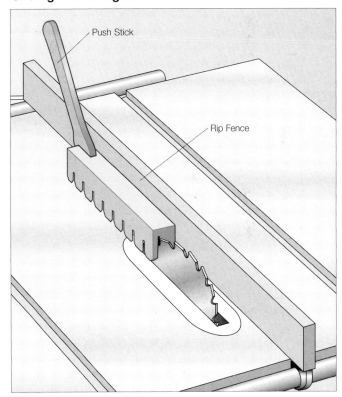

Watering Hole

Besides food, birds need water for bathing and drinking. The Watering Hole makes sure the birds get plenty of water for both.

Some birds will fly for miles to find a reliable source of clean water, so what could be more inviting than a yard with a watering hole/bath to go along with a source of food? The Watering Hole complements any bird feeder. By supplying birds with all their basic necessities in one location, you may encourage them to stay, build a nest in a nearby tree, and start a family.

This project has only a few parts and is easy to build. The water container is a pie tin set in a simple frame made from two boards and two cross supports. The wide wooden edge offers a safe platform for birds to dry their feathers and rest up before flying over to eat at one of the feeders you've built.

CUTTING & MATERIALS LIST

Part	Quantity	Dimensions	Part	Quantity	Dimensions
Platform	2	¾"x9¼"x18½"	Pie pan		9" diameter
Platform support	2	¾"x2"x13"	Glue		
Hangers	4	¾"x1½"x2¼"	Exterior enamel		
Deck screws	8	2¼" long	Cotton or nylon clothesline		
Deck screws	4	1¼" long			

Difficulty Level:

Overall View

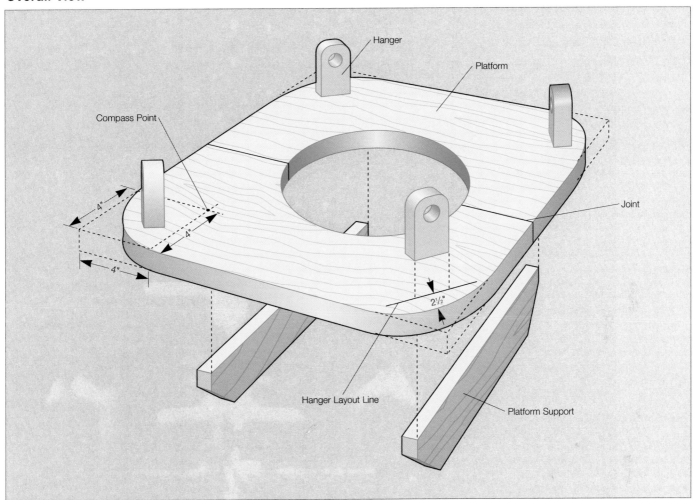

BUILDING THE WATERING HOLE

1 Assemble the Platform. Cut two pieces of 1x10 18½ inches long. With the grain running in the same direction, clamp the boards side by side to form an 18½-inch square. (Nominal 1x10 will already be 9¼ inches wide.) Draw diagonal layout lines across the corners of the square. The lines will cross at the exact center. Set a compass to a radius of 4½ inches. Place the compass point at the center of the platform and draw a circle. The 9-inch circle will hold the pie pan, which has a ⅜-inch lip.

Unclamp the boards and cut out the semicircles with a band saw, coping saw, or saber saw.

At each outside corner, draw 4-inch lines perpendicular to each side, 4 inches in from the corners. Set a compass at 4 inches, then place the point where the lines intersect. Draw the curves for the rounded corners, and cut along the curve lines with a coping saw or saber saw.

From each rounded corner, measure 2½ inches along the diagonal layout lines and make a mark. Using a combination square or protractor, draw a line across each corner that intersects the mark at 90 degrees. Later, you'll use these lines to position the hangers.

Assemble the platform with glue and clamps. When the glue cures, scrape off any excess.

2 Make the Platform Supports. Cut the 2x13-inch platform supports from one-by material. Using a combination square or protractor, lay out 45-degree cuts on each end of both supports as shown in Platform-Support and Hanger Layout. Note that the cuts start ½ inch from the top of each support. Make the cuts with a circular saw or handsaw.

3 Make the Hangers. Rip enough ¾-inch stock to 1½ inches wide to make the four hangers. Crosscut the stock to the hanger height of 2½ inches.

To round the tops of the hangers as shown in Platform-Support and Hanger Layout, set a compass to a ½-inch radius. Use a square to draw lines perpendicular to each side and ½ inch from the corners. Place the compass point where these lines intersect and draw the curves. Clamp the pieces to your workbench and make the cuts with a coping saw or saber saw.

Drill centered ¾-inch-diameter holes in the hangers as shown in Platform-Support and Hanger Layout. Using a rasp and sandpaper, round all the edges of the hangers, including the insides of the holes but excluding the bottom edges.

4   Rout the Platform and Supports. You'll rout the edges of the platform and the supports most easily on a router table. But you can also do the job safely with a hand-held router if you clamp the work securely to a bench. If you don't have a router, simply round the edges with a rasp and sandpaper.

First round-over all but the top edges of the supports with a ¼-inch roundover bit. Round-over the inside top edge of the platform hole.

Now lower the cutting depth to create a 1/16-inch lip as shown in Routing the Platform. Rout the top edges of the platform.

5   Attach the Platform Supports and Hangers. Position the platform supports across the glue joints and as close as possible to the hole in the platform as shown in the Overall View. Attach the supports with glue and countersunk 2¼-inch screws through the supports into the platform.

Platform-Support and Hanger Layout

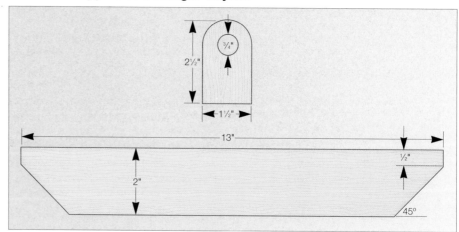

Routing the Platform

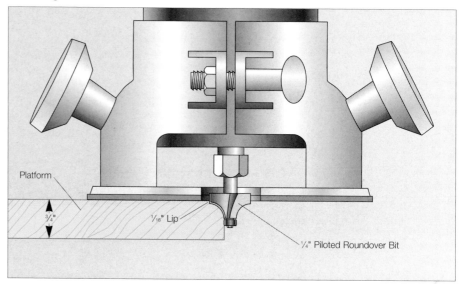

Fasten each hanger with one 1¼-inch screw driven through the bottom of the platform. To locate the positions of these screws, mark diagonal lines ⅜-inch in from the hanger-layout lines you made in Step 1. Drill a ⅛-inch hole at these four points. Counterbore the holes at the bottom of the platform. Put glue on the bottom of the hangers, center the hangers on the layout lines, then install the screws.

6   Finish the Watering Hole. Paint the project with exterior enamel or an epoxy finish so it will withstand rain as well as soaking by exuberant birds.

To hang the project, attach 24-inch lengths of cotton or nylon clothesline. Connect the lines to a ring or knot them together, then tie a separate line from that connecting point to a tree branch.

Bird~Feedosaurus

Dinky, a friendly-looking dinosaur that holds fruit, suet, or other bulk food, can be made from scrap lumber in a weekend with the kids.

Who says dinosaurs are extinct? Dinky the dinosaur, who represents the newly discovered species Bird-feedosaurus, certainly isn't.

Not only are kids fascinated with dinos, but the birds will be, too, when you entice them with a meal compliments of Dinky. Hang the feeder from a tree limb, set it on your deck railing, or place it on top of your picnic table. Stick a piece a fruit, such as an apple slice, on the skewer to attract orioles, mockingbirds, and sparrows, to name just a few. Try baking the apples to see if you can attract bluebirds and robins. Get creative and see what happens.

Made from a scrap 2x8 or larger piece of wood, this is a project that can be easily completed over a weekend.

CUTTING & MATERIALS LIST

Part	Quantity	Dimensions	Part	Quantity	Dimensions
Body	1	1½"x7¼"x12"	Screw eye	1	½" diameter
Dowel perches	2	¼" diameter x5"	Glue		
Dowel skewer	1	¼" diameter x7"	Paint		
Wood ball	1	¾" diameter			

Difficulty Level:

Overall View

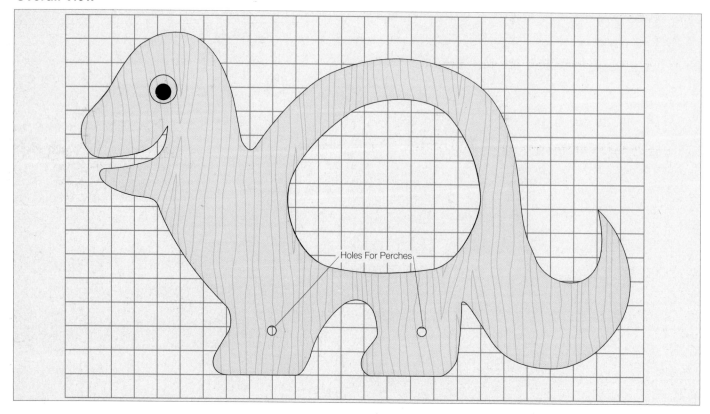

Holes For Perches

BUILDING THE FEEDER

1 Cut Out the Body.

The dinosaur pattern is shown 50 percent of actual size. Increase it to full size by reproducing the pattern on a photocopier set to 200 percent. Or sketch your own dinosaur, if you like. Cut out the pattern and tape it to a piece of 2x8. You can cut the overall shape and inner section with a coping saw or saber saw. Drill a starter hole and cut out the center section before cutting out the rest of the shape.

Using a rasp and sandpaper or a router equipped with a ¼-inch roundover bit, round the edges of both sides of the feeder. Sand the project with 100-grit sandpaper.

2 Drill the Skewer and Perch Holes.

Clamp the feeder securely in a bench or machine vise. Use padding with the machine vise and be careful not to mar the wood. Use a ¼-inch bit to drill through the top edge only.

Reposition the feeder in the clamp so you can drill the two ¼-inch perch holes as shown on the pattern. To prevent the drill bit from tearing the wood as it comes out the other side, clamp a piece of scrap to your feeder in the area of the exit hole.

3 Make the Perches and Skewer.

Cut two ¼-inch-diameter dowels 5 inches long to serve as the perches, and one 7 inches long for the skewer. Center the perches in the holes so that approximately 1¾ inches protrudes from each side of the feeder. Glue the perches in place.

Sharpen one end of the skewer and stick it through the drilled hole on the top portion of the body. Mark where the point meets the other side. Notch out a hole for the skewer point with a fine chisel, or drill a hole with a ¼-inch bit that's at least 6 inches long. The hole needs to be only ¼ inch deep.

Place the wood ball in a vise or clamp and drill a ¼-inch hole into the ball (as explained in the Hanging Apples feeder, on page 19). Glue the ball to the skewer.

4 Finish the Feeder.

Attach the screw eye as shown in the photo and paint the project the color(s) of your choice.

NOTE: *Over time, juice from the fruit may expand the skewer, making it difficult to insert the skewer back into the feeder. If this expansion happens, sand the skewer down until it fits snugly.*

Bird Feeder/ Robin's Roost
Page 63

Gazebo Rest Stop
Page 91

Swiss Chalet
Page 14

Squirrel Feeder
Page 74

Tin~Can Seed Shoppe
Page 68

Pig Bird Feeder
Page 82

Bird~Feedosaurus
Page 31

Multilevel Seed Silo
Page 71

Seed Bell Shelter
Page 78

Feline Feeding Stand
Page 54

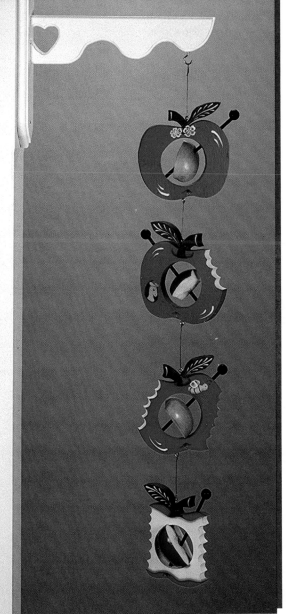

Hanging Apples
Page 19

Milk~Jug Seed Depot
Page 46

Cozy Cottage
Page 51

Chickadee Feeder
Page 48

Watering Hole
Page 28

Thistle Seed Dispenser
Page 87

Seed, Suet, and Water Station
Page 41

Seed and Suet Storehouse
Page 58

Suet Holder
Page 24

Seed, Suet, and Water Station

Designed to cover a range of needs, the Seed, Suet, and Water Station will have a little something to satisfy every bird in your yard.

This is the birds' equivalent of a corner convenience store—open all night and day with lots to offer in a small space. This feeding station offers a wire-mesh suet chamber, an acrylic seed chamber, and a water container.

A small pie pan or any kind of bowl that fits in the hole will work fine as the water container. Birds will appreciate the water in areas where it's hard to find. Watch how the water bowl keeps the birds coming back for more—so keep it filled.

Suet is especially welcome by insect-eating birds in the winter, when bugs are scarce at best. The suet supplements the birds' diet with fat and protein. When it's not cold enough outside to keep suet from spoiling, put bread in the suet feeder. Mash the bread against the mesh so the birds can get at it.

Because it offers something for everyone in the feathered world, the Seed, Suet, and Water Station is a great way to attract a wide variety of birds to your yard.

CUTTING & MATERIALS LIST

Part	Quantity	Dimensions
Base	1	½"x12"x20¾"
Water-bowl retainer	1	½"x8" diameter with 6½" hole
Base end trim	2	½"x1"x13½"
Base side trim	2	½"x1"x22¼"
Roof posts	4	¾"x1¼"x11"
Feed chamber sides	4	¾"x2½"x8"
Feed chamber tops	4	¾"x⅝"x5"
Feed chamber lids	2	¾"x2½"x6½"
Lid inserts	2	¾"x1¼"x4⅞"
Feed chamber diverters	2	1½"x1½"x5"
Long roof section	1	¾"x7¼"x21"
Short roof section	1	¾"x6½"x21"
Gable trim	2	¾" thick, cut to shape
Roof trim	14	¼"x¾"x6¾"
Wide ridge trim	2	¼"x1"x10¾"
Wide ridge trim	2	¼"x1"x12½"
Narrow ridge trim	2	¼"x¾"x10¾"

Part	Quantity	Dimensions
Narrow ridge trim	2	¼"x¾"x12½"
Chimney	1	1½"x3½"x5"
Chimney plaque	2	⅜" thick, cut to shape
Deck screws		1⅝" long
Deck screws		1¼" long
Deck screws		1" long
Brads		¾" long
Screw eyes	2	1" diameter
¼" Wire mesh sheets	2	5½" wide x 7½" long
Wood plugs		Sized to fit countersink
Water container	1	Small pie pan or something similar
Acrylic panels	2	5½" wide x 6¾" long
Glue		
Silicone sealant		
Paint or stain		

Difficulty Level:

BUILDING THE FEEDER

1 Make the Base. Cut the ½-inch plywood base 12 inches wide and 20¾ inches long. Use a compass to lay out a 6½-inch-diameter circle in the center of the base. (Draw a circle to match the water container you plan to use.) Drill a starter hole in the circle, then cut the hole with a keyhole saw or saber saw.

Make the water-bowl retainer of ½-inch plywood, as well. Lay out a circle of the same diameter as the hole you cut in the base, then reset the compass for a diameter that's 1½ inches bigger. Lay out this bigger circle around the first circle, then cut out the retainer. Round the top edges of the retainer with a rasp and sandpaper. Use glue and counter-sunk 1-inch screws to secure the water-bowl retainer around the hole.

Cut the base trim to the dimensions in the Cutting List. It will fit around the perimeter of the base with 45-degree miters at the corners. Make the cuts with a miter box.

2 Make the Feed Chamber Sides and Rails. The sides and top rails of the feed chamber have grooves along their length to

Making the Feed Chamber Sides and Rails

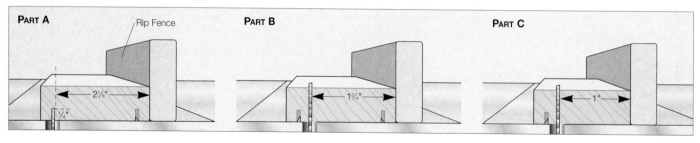

PART A — Rip Fence — 2⅛" — ¼"

PART B — 1¾"

PART C — 1"

Overall View

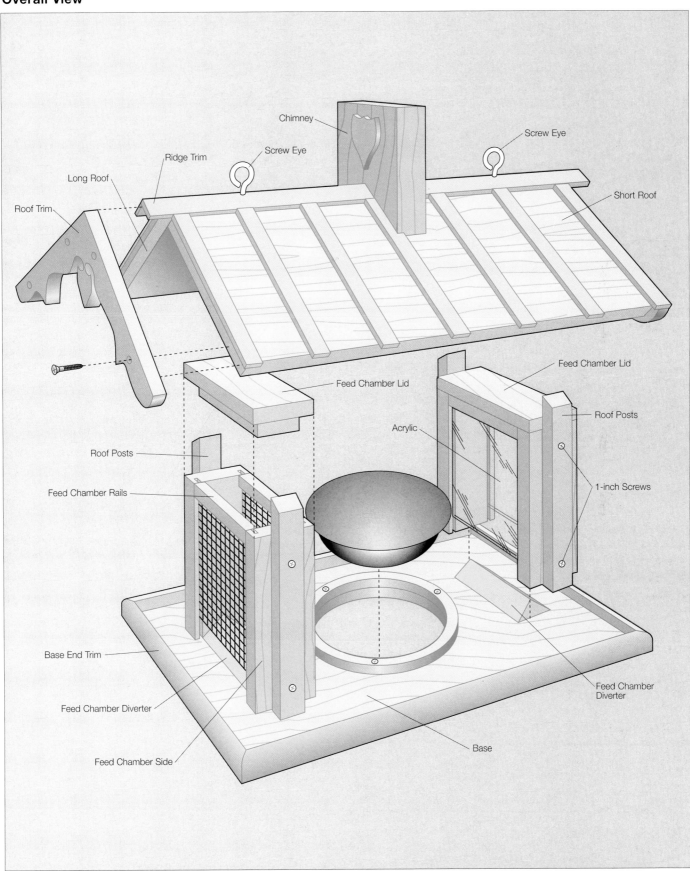

Chimney

Screw Eye

Screw Eye

Ridge Trim

Long Roof

Short Roof

Roof Trim

Feed Chamber Lid

Feed Chamber Lid

Roof Posts

Acrylic

Roof Posts

1-inch Screws

Feed Chamber Rails

Base End Trim

Feed Chamber Diverter

Feed Chamber Diverter

Feed Chamber Side

Base

receive the acrylic or wire-mesh fronts and backs. Rip the pieces and cut the grooves on a table saw. The procedure described below is the safest way to do this. Be sure to use a push stick when making the grooves and rip cuts.

Cut a piece of 1x3 (actual dimensions: ¾x2½ inches) 44 inches long. Set the table-saw blade to ¼ inch above the table as shown in Part A of Making the Feed Chamber Sides and Rails. Set the rip fence to 2⅛ inches from the blade. Run the piece of stock over the blade then flip it around and groove the other side of the same face as shown.

From the grooved stock, crosscut four pieces, each 8 inches long. These are the feed chamber sides.

Set the rip fence 1¾ inches from the blade and raise the blade to cut through the stock as shown in Part B of Making the Feed Chamber Sides and Rails. Run the stock through the blade. The narrow piece that falls off will make two top rails.

To make the other top rails, set the saw blade 1 inch from the fence as a shown in Part C of Making the Feed Chamber Sides and Rails. Rip off the other grooved side. Now crosscut all four top rails 5 inches long.

3 Assemble the Feed Chambers.
Cut one piece of solid wood to 1½x1½x12 inches long, minimum, for the feed chamber seed diverters. (The extra length is for safety.) Tilt the table-saw blade 45 degrees, and using a push stick, rip the piece diagonally in two as shown in Cutting the Seed Diverters. Each triangle will be about 1 inch high and 2 inches wide at the base.

Position the feed chamber diverters on the base, 3½ inches from the base sides and 2 inches from each end. Predrill and attach the diverters with 1⅝-inch screws driven on an

Cutting the Seed Diverters

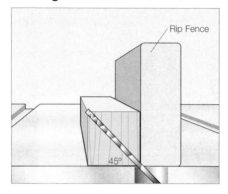

angle through them and into the base. Align the feed chamber sides against the ends of the seed diverters. Screw the sides into the ends of the diverters using 1¼-inch screws.

To make the feed chamber widows, cut the acrylic panels and wire mesh to fit into the feed chamber grooves. Slip the two pieces of wire mesh into the side grooves of one chamber. Fit the top rails onto the top of the mesh pieces. You can pull these top rails off to stuff suet or bread into the chamber.

Slip the acrylic pieces into the grooves in the other chamber and put the rails in place. There will be a gap at the bottom for seed to slip through. With a ⅛-inch bit, drill holes into the sides of the grooves and through the acrylic in the groove as shown in the Overall View. Insert brads into the holes to pin the acrylic in place. Remove the top rails, squirt some silicone into the grooves, then reinstall them on the acrylic. The silicone will serve as a gasket to prevent the plastic from rattling.

Now cut the feed chamber lids and lid inserts to the dimensions in the Cutting List. Center the lid inserts under the feed chamber lids and secure them with glue and 1¼-inch screws as shown in the Overall View. Round the top edges of the lids with a ¼-inch roundover bit in a router or with a rasp and sandpaper. Put the lids in place.

4 Make and Install the Roof and Chimney.
Cut the roof posts to the dimensions in the Cutting List, beveling one end of each post at 45 degrees to meet the roof. Center the posts on the chamber sides and attach them with glue and countersunk 1-inch screws as shown in the Overall View.

Cut the roof pieces from one-by material to the dimensions in the Cutting List. Place the long roof over the short roof as shown in the Overall View and assemble them with 1¼-inch screws. Center the roof assembly over the posts and secure it with countersunk 1¼-inch screws into each post.

Cut the chimney to the dimensions in the Cutting List. Use a handsaw or saber saw to notch the block as shown in the Overall View. The chimney plaque is, of course, optional. If you want to include the plaque, make a copy of the pattern provided in Trim Patterns on a photocopy machine set at 200 percent. If you can't get access to an enlarging photocopier, use the grid to create your own pattern. Cut out the pattern and attach it to ⅜-inch stock, then cut the wood with a band saw, coping saw, or scroll saw. Attach the plaque to the chimney with glue. Locate the chimney on the ridge, 9 inches from one end of the roof. Predrill and attach the chimney by driving a 1⅝-inch screw up through the roof and into the center of the chimney.

5 Cut and Install the Trim for the Roof.
Make two gable trim patterns as shown in Trim Patterns and discussed above. Cut out the patterns and tape them to pieces of one-by wood. Cut out the trim with a band saw, saber saw, or scroll saw. Round the top edges of the two pieces with a ¼-inch roundover bit in a router or with a rasp and sandpaper. Secure the

Trim Patterns

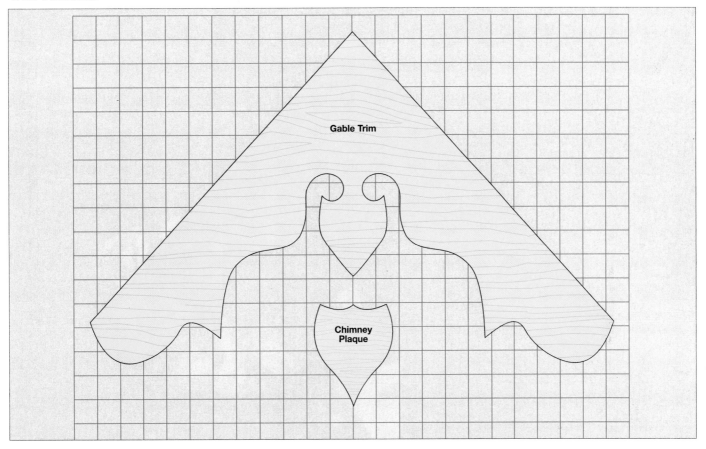

gable trim to the roof with counter-sunk 1¼-inch screws and glue. Fill the holes with wood plugs and sand them smooth.

Cut the ridge trim and roof trim to the dimensions in the Cutting List. Position the ridge trim on the roof so that the wide pieces overlap the narrow pieces as shown in the Overall View. Fasten the trim with glue and brads.

Measure ⅜ inch from the gable end of the roof on each side and set four pieces of roof trim with brads. Lay the 10 remaining pieces of trim, leaving a 2¾-inch space between each. The trim should cover the screws holding the roof to the four posts. Notch the two pieces of trim that meet the chimney to fit around it, beveling the horizontal cut 45 degrees for a snug fit.

6 **Finish the Feeder.** Drill two ¼-inch holes down into the roof and attach the 2⅛-inch screw eyes as shown in the Overall View. Paint or stain the project the color(s) of your choice.

Milk~Jug Seed Depot

Put an empty plastic 1-gal. milk container to use by crafting this easy-to-make bird feeder. The real fun comes in being as creative as you wish with your paint job.

This simple feeder, made from a 1-gallon milk jug, is a great project to do with children because it requires just a few tools. The kids may need a little help or supervision from a grown-up for the cutting and drilling, but then you can let them nail the project together and have a blast painting it with their own design.

The feeder is especially suited to smaller birds that can hop inside the opening. Do your best to make sure that the feeder is squirrel-proof; a furry thief that makes it to the perch can easily tip the feeder and spill out the seed.

CUTTING & MATERIALS LIST

Part	Quantity	Dimensions		Part	Quantity	Dimensions
Wood Insert	1	¾"x3"x6"		Glue		
Perch	1	¼" diameter x3" long		Wire, Chain, or Fishing Line		
Plastic Gallon Milk Jug	1			Paint		
Brads	3	¾" long				

Difficulty Level:

BUILDING THE FEEDER

1 Prepare the Container. Thoroughly clean the milk jug with soap and warm water. If you have difficulty removing the labels, try soaking the jug in hot water.

Next, you'll want to cut a hole. Milk containers vary somewhat in shape, but refer to the Overall View to give you a general idea of how to cut the hole. Use a pair of scissors to do the cutting.

2 Make and Install the Wood Insert. Using the piece you cut out of the milk jug as a guide, trace the bottom portion of the opening onto a 3x6-inch piece of one-by wood. Cut the wood to shape using a coping saw or saber saw. When making the insert, be sure you don't plug up the opening too much. Leave the hole about two-thirds open so the birds will have room to fly in and out.

Cut a ¼-inch-diameter dowel 3 inches long to serve as the perch. Drill a ¼-inch-diameter hole in the wood insert, positioning the hole just high of center. Attach the dowel with a dab of glue to keep it in place. Place the wood insert in the opening, then nail three brads through the jug into the insert's sides to keep it in place.

3 Drill the Hanging Holes. To balance the bird feeder properly, drill a ¼-inch-diameter hole at the base of the handle as

Overall View

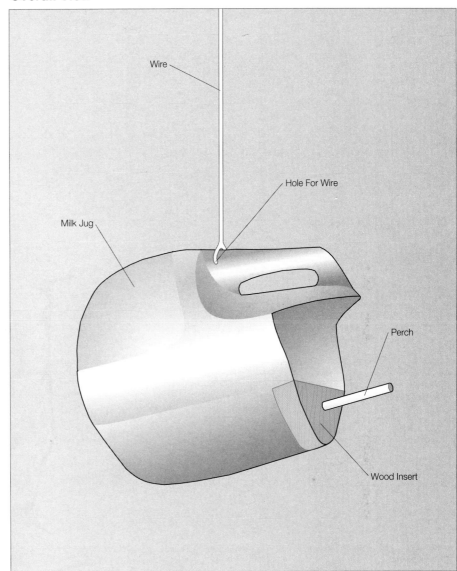

shown in the Overall View. If you don't have a drill, punch a hole in the jug using an awl or the point of a pair of scissors.

4 Finish the Feeder. Paint the project with leaves, flowers, or any motif you like. Don't paint the feeder a dark hue because the color will absorb sunlight and overheat the interior. When the paint is dry, attach the fishing line, wire, or chain, and hang the bird feeder.

Chickadee Feeder

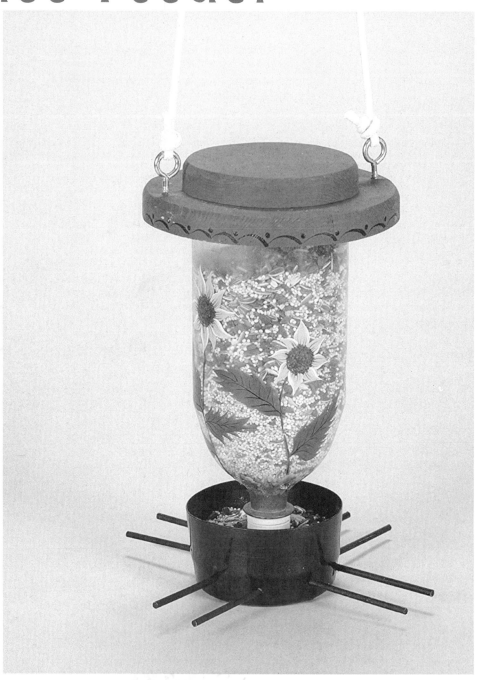

A 2-liter soda bottle, some scrap lumber, and a few wooden dowels make for a feeder that's made to order for chickadees.

Y ou'll make friends with small birds, especially chickadees, if you put out this feeder. The main body of the feeder is a 2-liter soda bottle with small holes drilled near the bottom. The holes are perfectly suited to the chickadee lifestyle because the birds like to pluck out one seed, then fly to a nearby branch to eat. You may notice a small group of the tiny birds on branches near the feeder. This is because chickadees have a "pecking order"; each perches patiently on a nearby branch awaiting its turn at the food source.

By using the parts of a plastic soda bottle to make the feeder, you'll perform a nifty bit of recycling by transforming trash into something attractive.

CUTTING & MATERIALS LIST

Part	Quantity	Dimensions	Part	Quantity	Dimensions
Bottle-Holding Board	1	¾"x7" diameter	Brads		1" long
Outer Lid	1	¾"x4¾" diameter	Deck Screw		¾" long
Inner Lid	1	¾"x4¼"diameter (diameter of your bottle)	Deck Screw		1¼" long
Seed Platform	1	¾"x4⅛" diameter (dia. of bottle bottom)	Screw Eyes	2	½" diameter
			Wire or Small Chain		
Perches	4	¼" diameter x10" long	Paint		
Soda Bottle	1	2-liter size			

Difficulty Level:

BUILDING THE FEEDER

1 **Clean, Disassemble, and Cut the Bottle.** Rinse out the soda bottle with hot, soapy water. The hot water will both clean the bottle and help remove any labels. The bottom piece is attached with hot-melt adhesive, so the hot water should soften the glue enough for you to pull it off. Save the bottom piece and the cap for Steps 4 and 5.

Measure approximately 10 inches from the bottle opening to the bottom of the bottle. You may find it helpful to mark the 10-inch distance at several points around the circumference of the bottle. Cut off the bottom using a pair of scissors or a utility knife.

2 **Make and Attach the Bottle-Holding Board.** The bottle-holding board is a circular piece of wood with an outside diameter of 7 inches. It has a 4¼-inch-diameter hole (your bottle diameter may be slightly larger or smaller) in the middle designed to receive the cut end of the bottle.

To make the board, use a compass to draw a 7-inch circle on a 1x8. Cut

Overall View

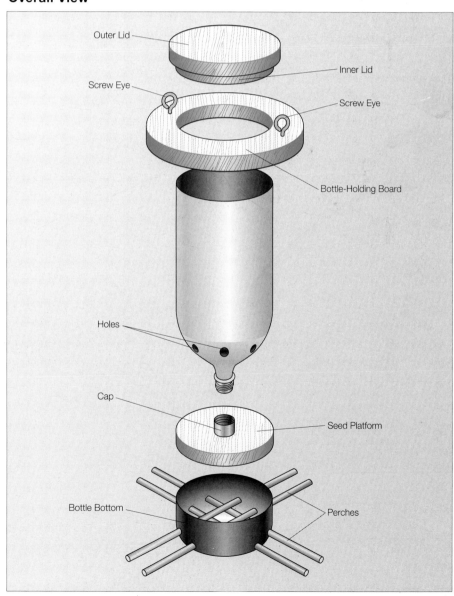

Outer Lid

Inner Lid

Screw Eye

Screw Eye

Bottle-Holding Board

Holes

Cap

Seed Platform

Bottle Bottom

Perches

Cutting a Circle

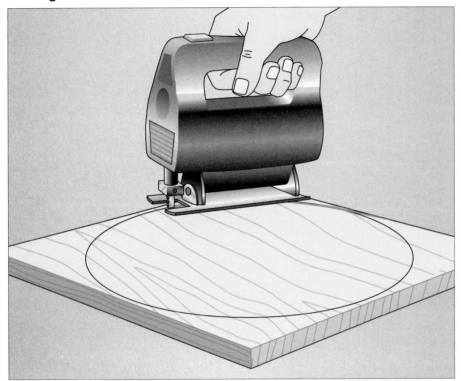

the circle with a coping saw or saber saw. Next, center the bottom of the bottle on the circle. Trace around the outside of the bottle to lay out the hole. Cut the hole with a saber saw by first drilling a ½-inch hole inside the cutout, just touching the layout line. Use the ½-inch hole as the starting hole for the saber saw. If you don't have a saber saw, you can make the cut with a coping saw by detaching the blade, threading the blade through the hole, then reattaching the blade. Round-over the top edge of the holding board with a rasp and sandpaper or a router equipped with a roundover bit. Attach the bottle to the inside of this board using four brads.

3   Make the Outer and Inner Lids. Use a compass to lay out the outer and inner lids according to the dimensions in the Cutting List. Cut the lids from one-by stock. Center the inner lid on the bottom of the outer lid and fasten it with one 1¼-inch screw and glue. Round-over the top edge of the lid assembly.

4   Make and Attach the Seed Platform. Lay out the 4⅛-inch diameter (or the diameter of the inside of your soda-bottle bottom piece) of the seed platform. Cut the platform with a coping saw or saber saw. Set the board inside

the detached soda-bottle bottom with four evenly spaced brads nailed through the sides of the bottom into the board. Leave room under the platform to insert the wood dowels.

Drill a ⅛-inch hole in the center of the soda bottle cap. Use a ¾-inch screw to attach the cap to the center of the seed platform. Drill four ¼-inch-diameter holes evenly spaced around the soda bottle just under the neck. Screw the bottle onto the cap.

5   Attach the Perches. The wood perches consist of four dowels that pass through the old bottle bottom, under the seed platform. Drill holes through one side of the plastic piece and out the other side so that the holes will be aligned. Make sure two sets of holes are above the other two sets so that one pair of dowels can pass over the other pair. Cut the dowels 10 inches long and push them through the holes.

6   Finish the Feeder. Attach two screw eyes and wire or chain to the sides of the bottle-holder board. Now's the time to paint your feeder, if you wish. To avoid "cooking" the birdseed, don't use too many dark colors when decorating your feeder. Also, if you leave most of the sides unpainted, you'll be able to tell when your feeder needs more seed.

Fill the bird feeder with seed, put the lid on, and hang it from your favorite tree or on your back porch.

Cozy Cottage

Birds are welcome to this house to eat the fruit, bread, or suet left in the windows and door.

Small birds will feel right at home when they visit this feeder designed to look like a cottage. A few tacked-on accessories and a clever paint scheme help conceal the simplicity of this project. The Cozy Cottage feeder, complete with awning, window boxes, and chimney, can be built with a table saw, a few hand tools, and a few pieces of scrap wood. If you like, you can try to duplicate the look and style of your own home—or a friend's, for a unique and personal gift.

Almost any grain or fruit-based food will attract chickadees, finches, and sparrows to your yard. Place a leftover sandwich in the feeder's doorway as a welcome mat. Then look out a window in your house and watch the birds perch on the feeder's window sills.

Cutting & Materials List

Part	Quantity	Dimensions	Part	Quantity	Dimensions
House	1	¾"x7¼"x10"	Door skewer	1	¼" diameter x2"
Chimney	1	¾"x1½"x2"	Window skewer	1	¼" diameter x3"
Top flower box	1	¾"x¾"x2"	Chimney skewer	1	¼" diameter x5"
Bottom flower box	1	¾"x¾"x3"	Brads	4	¾" long
Doorstep	1	¾"x¾"x2"	Screw eyes	2	½" diameter
Awning	1	¾"x1⅛"x2"	Wire or fishing line		
Roof (long)	1	¼"x1¾"x6"	Glue		
Roof (short)	1	¼"x1¾"x5¾"	Paint		

Difficulty Level:

Building the Feeder

1 Lay Out and Cut the House.
Make the body of the house from a piece of 1x8 cut 10 inches long. The Overall View provides all the dimensions you need to lay out the two windows and the door. Center the top window from side to side, and lay out the 1¼-inch radius of its arch with a compass.

Cut the window and door openings before you cut the roof pitch. Start each opening by drilling a ¼-inch starter hole. Then cut out the shapes with a coping saw or saber saw. Cut the roof line (a centered 90-degree angle) with a handsaw or saber saw.

2 Make and Install the Accessories. You'll cut the awning, doorstep, and flower boxes all from one piece of ¾-inch-thick stock. The drawing Accessory Profiles shows how to lay out the beveled sides of the awning and window boxes. Start with a piece of stock that's at least 18 inches long (longer than you need to make the pieces but the minimum you need to rip safely on the table saw). Rip the piece to 1⅛ inches wide, then

Overall View

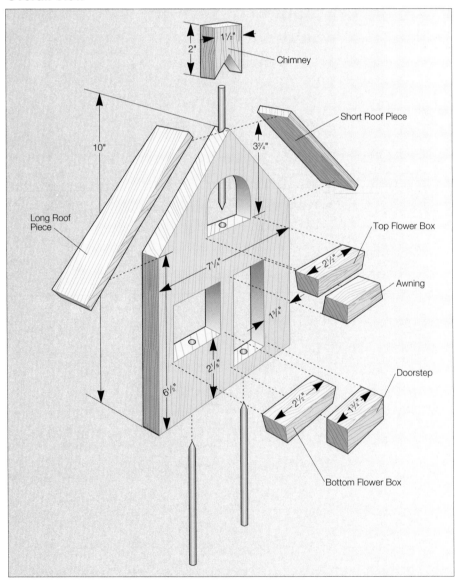

Accessory Profiles

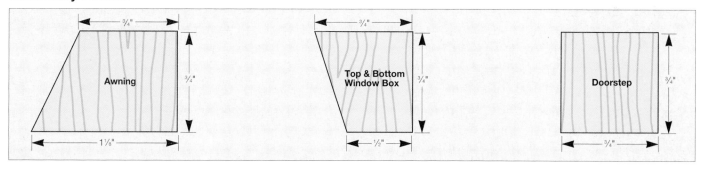

lay out the bevel for the awning. Tilt your table-saw blade to match the bevel angle and rip the whole strip. Then cut off the 2-inch length you need for the awning.

Now rip the piece down to ¾ inches for the doorstep and window boxes. Cut a piece 2 inches long for the doorstep. Lay out the bevel for the window boxes, and adjust the saw-blade angle. Rip the whole piece, then cut the length you need for the two window boxes. Glue and clamp the accessories into place.

3 Make and Install the Roof. Cut the chimney and roof pieces to the dimensions in the Cutting List. Notch the chimney as shown in Overall View and put it aside for the time being. Assemble the roof pieces with glue and brads,

positioning them so that the long piece overlaps the short one.

4 Install the Skewers. Cut the three skewers from ¼-inch dowel material to the dimensions in the Cutting List. Sharpen one end of each skewer with a pencil sharpener. Drill ¼-inch holes for the two lower skewers through the bottom of the house into the door and lower-window openings. Put some glue in the holes and tap the dowels into place from the bottom of the house with the sharp ends pointing up.

For the upper window you'll attach the skewer to the chimney. This way, you can insert the skewer and remove it by pushing the chimney on and pulling it off. Drill a ¼-inch hole down through the peak of the roof, and continue drilling until you make

a ¼-inch-deep hole in the bottom of the window. Drill a ½-inch-deep hole in the bottom of the chimney, then glue the dowel into the hole with the sharp end pointing down. Now you'll be able to stick a piece of food in the window, and poke the skewer through the hole in the roof and right through the food.

5 Finish the Feeder. Paint the house to suit your taste, attach the screw eyes and wire or fishing line to the roof, and hang the feeder where you can watch the small visitors eat their fill.

NOTE: *Over time, juice from the fruit may expand the skewer, making it difficult to insert the skewer back into the feeder. If this expansion happens, sand the skewer down until it fits snugly.*

Feline Feeding Stand

A discarded juice jar containing birdseed makes this tomcat a welcome sight to birds.

Meet the one cat the birds in your neighborhood will flock to when they want a bite to eat—and not the other way around. This old tomcat houses a juice jar that dispenses all the birdseed your feathered neighbors can eat.

The feeder is made by laminating layers of wood to give the cat a more lifelike shape. Be sure to use a waterproof glue throughout the project, or the first rainy day could be a cat-astrophe!

CUTTING & MATERIALS LIST

Part	Quantity	Dimensions	Part	Quantity	Dimensions
Face	1	¾"x6½"x7"	Perch dowels	2	¼" diameter x13½"
Neck	1	¾"x5"x4"	Bird-support dowel	1	¼" diameter x1"
Front	1	¾"x6"x9½"	Post cleats	2	¾"x¾"x5"
Rear	1	¾"x6"x16"	Ribbon	1	24"
Nose	1	¼"x1½"x1¼"	Deck screws		1¼"
Heart pendant	1	¼"x2¾"x3¼"	Deck screws		1⅝"
Bird	1	¾"x3½"x7½"	Brads		1"
Bottle Holder	1	¾"x5½"x7"	Wood plugs	12	Sized to fit the countersink
Base	1	¾"x7½"x12"			
Base ends	2	¾"x1"x10½"	Juice bottle	1	32 to 40 oz.
Feed chamber sides	2	½"x½"x7"	Soda bottle bottom		2-liter size
Feed chamber ends	2	½"x½"x5"	Paint		
Bottle lifters	2	½"x½"x4"			

Difficulty Level:

BUILDING THE FEEDER

1 **Make and Cut Out the Patterns.** The patterns shown are 50 percent of their actual size. To make them full-size, reproduce them on a photocopier set at 200 percent. Of course, you don't have to copy these patterns precisely. You can sketch your own designs if you like. Cut the patterns out and use tape or contact adhesive to place them directly onto your stock. If you plan to make multiple copies of the feeder, glue the patterns to thicker paperboard or make permanent patterns of hardboard.

Cut out the face, neck, front, back, nose, bird, and heart pendant using a band saw, coping saw, or saber saw. Make all of the pieces from one-by lumber except for the heart pendant and the nose, which you'll make from ¼-inch plywood.

Overall View

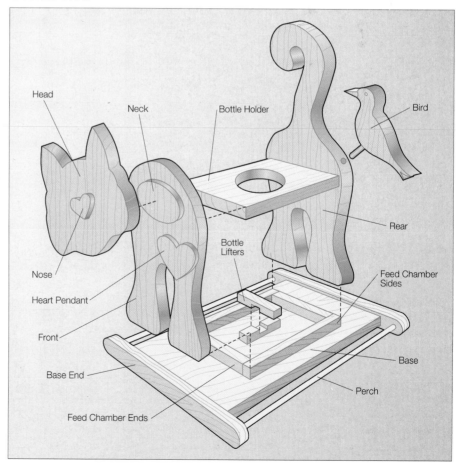

Head

Neck

Bottle Holder

Bird

Nose

Heart Pendant

Front

Base End

Feed Chamber Ends

Bottle Lifters

Rear

Feed Chamber Sides

Base

Perch

With a router and a ¼-inch round-over bit, rout both sides of the front and rear body sections, both sides of the tail, and the front of the face. Sand the edges and sides of the boards with 100-grit sandpaper. Round the edges of the nose with sandpaper, and use sandpaper to smooth the edges of the heart pendant and the bird.

2 Make the Bottle Holder. The bottle holder is a 1x6 cut 7 inches long. Round-over both edges of the long sides with the ¼-inch roundover bit. Cut a hole in the center of the holder to match the diameter of the bottle you'll use. To make the hole, drill a ¼-inch starter hole on the inside edge of the circle, then cut out the circle with a coping saw or saber saw.

3 Assemble the Cat. Draw a line 7 inches up from the feet on the inside of both the front and rear sections. Align the bottom edge of the bottle holder with these lines. Attach the front and tail sections to the bottle holder using countersunk 1⅝-inch screws and glue.

Nail the nose onto the face using two brads. Glue and screw the neck and face to the front section. When placing screws, be careful not to position one screw on top of another in the layer beneath. Fill the visible screw holes with wood plugs and sand them smooth.

4 Make the Base and Perches. Cut the base and base ends to the dimensions in the Cutting List. Round the cut sides of the base ends with a rasp and sandpaper or a belt sander. Round-over both edges of the long sides of the base with a ¼-inch roundover bit in the router. Drill holes for the wood-dowel perches in the base ends. Counterbore holes for two 1¼-inch screws into each base end. Apply glue to the ends of the dowels and slip them into the holes in the base

Front and Back Patterns

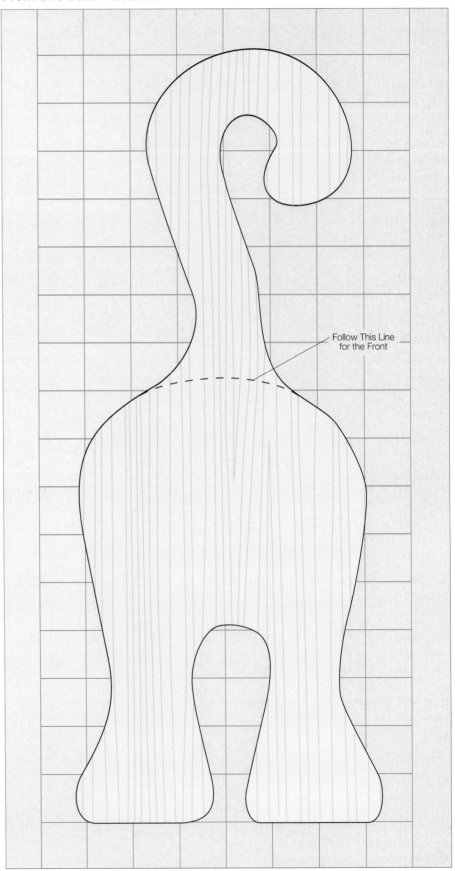

Follow This Line for the Front

Head, Neck, Heart-Pendant, and Nose Patterns

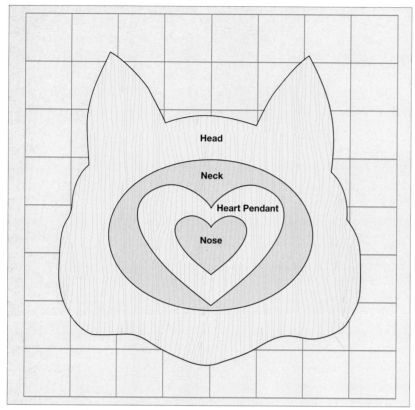

Bird Pattern

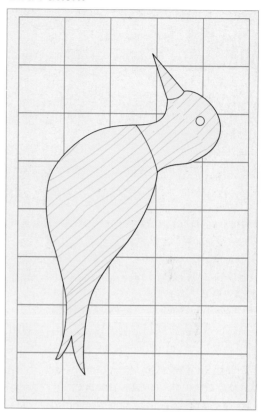

ends. Put glue on the ends of the base and slip the dowel-and-base-end assemblies into place. Insert the screws, then sand the entire base.

5 Attach the Cat Assembly to the Base. Center the cat on the base and mark the positions of the paws. Using the marks as a guide, drill holes down from the top, then countersink these holes on the bottom side of the base. Drive four 1⅝-inch screws through the bottom of the base and into the cat's paws.

6 Install the Feed Chamber Sides and Lifters. Cut the feed chamber sides and ends to the dimensions in the Cutting List. Lay out these pieces on the base so that the bottle will be centered in the feed chamber. Attach the pieces to the base with glue and brads.

The bottle lifters cross each other with a small half-lap joint. Cut the lifters to the dimensions in the Cutting List. Use a handsaw to kerf the notched area ¾ inch wide by ¼ inch deep, then clean out the notch with a ¾-inch chisel. Center the lifters in the feed chamber before attaching them with glue and brads.

7 Complete the Feeder. You're going to attach the bird on top of the tail using a ¼x1-inch wood dowel. Drill a ¼-inch-diameter hole ⅝ inch deep into the cat's tail, then into the bird. Wrap a piece of tape around your drill bit as a depth gauge as shown in Depth-Stop Gauge. Apply glue to both ends of the dowel and stick it in place.

Paint the entire bird feeder as desired. Drill a ¼-inch-diameter hole in the heart pendant, then thread a ribbon through the pen-

dant hole and hang the heart around the cat's neck.

Detach the black plastic bottom from a 2-liter soda bottle. Fill the juice jar with seed, place it upside-down on the feeder, and cover the jar with the black plastic bottom to protect it from the weather.

You can attach the feeder to a 4x4 post using ¾x¾-inch cleats. Screw the cleats to the top of the post, on opposite sides, with 1⅝-inch screws, then the base to the cleats using 1¼-inch screws.

Depth-Stop Gauge

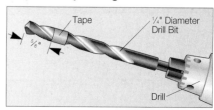

Seed and Suet Storehouse

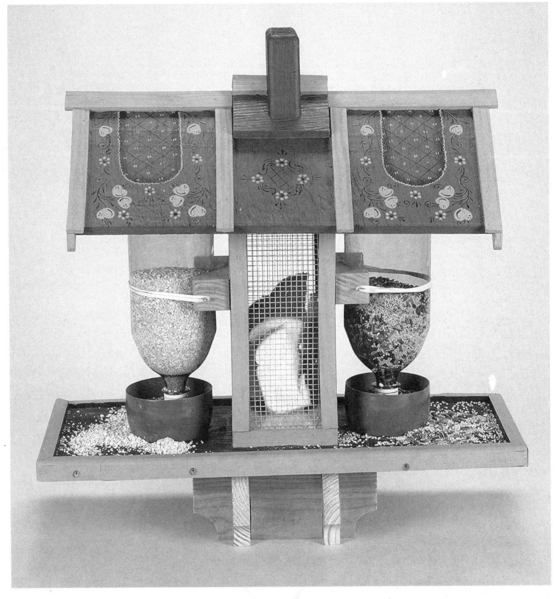

With the capability of holding two kinds of seed and suet or bread, the Seed and Suet Storehouse will appeal to a wide variety of bird species.

Although it may be impossible to satisfy the many hundreds of species of birds with a single feeder, this one makes a gallant attempt by offering a smorgasbord in hope of attracting as many birds as possible.

Each species has different likes and dislikes. You may notice that some foods will attract certain species by the flock. But put out something different, and the birds you once enjoyed watching may stay away, leaving the food untouched. For this reason, the Seed and Suet Storehouse is designed to hold different kinds of food: By housing suet and birdseed holders, the feeder displays a little something for a variety of birds. Put tiny seeds like millet or thistle in one seed holder and sunflower seeds or chopped nuts in the other, and you'll attract small birds like goldfinches and chickadees as well as larger cardinals, grosbeaks, and woodpeckers. The suet will help attract many insect-eating birds, such as flickers, bluebirds, and wrens, especially in the winter.

Remember that suet tends to spoil in warm weather, so substitute bread or fruit in the center feeder during the summer months. Be sure to push the food against the wire mesh in the compartment so the birds can peck at it easily.

CUTTING & MATERIALS LIST

Part	Quantity	Dimensions
Base Assembly		
Base	1	½"x9"x22"
Base end trim	2	¾"x1"x10½"
Base side trim	2	¾"x1"x23½"
Post wrap	4	¾"x4"x9"
Suet Chamber		
Sides	2	½"x5½"x15"
Top blocks	2	½"x3"x4"
Tilt board (long)	1	½"x4½"x4"
Tilt board (short)	1	½"x4"x4"
Horizontal trim	4	¼"x¾"x5"
Vertical trim	4	¼"x¾"x9¾"
Bottle supports	2	1½"x1¾"x5½"
Seed platform	2	¾"x4¼" diameter
Roof		
Long roof section	1	½"x8"x19½"
Short roof section	1	½"x7½"x19½"
Wide ridge trim	2	¼"x¾"x8¼"
Narrow ridge trim	2	¼"x½"x8¼"
Vertical trim	8	¼"x¾"x7¾"
Roof rake	2	¼"x13"x6"

Part	Quantity	Dimensions
Chimney cap		
Long roof side	1	½"x3"x4½"
Short roof side	1	½"x2½"x4½"
Long cap block	1	½"x1½"x3"
Short cap block	1	½"x1"x3"
Wide chimney ridge trim	2	¼"x¾"x1⅝"
Narrow chimney ridge trim	2	¼"x½"x1⅝"
Chimney	1	1½"x3½"x3¾"
Soda bottle	2	2-liter size
¼" Wire mesh	2	5" wide x10½" long
Deck screws		¾" long
Deck screws		1" long
Deck screws		1⅝" long
Deck screws		2½" long
Brads		⅞" long
Cup hooks	4	¾" diameter
Rubber bands	4	
Paint		
Wire or small chain		

Difficulty Level:

BUILDING THE FEEDER

1 Make the Base and Post Wrap. Cut the base and trim pieces to the dimensions in the Cutting List. Miter-cut the trim pieces at 45 degrees. Attach the trim flush to the bottom of the base so it forms a lip to hold the seed. Fasten the trim with glue and countersunk 1¼-inch screws. Round the edges of the trim with a rasp and sandpaper or a ¼-inch roundover bit in a router.

Post-Wrap Layout

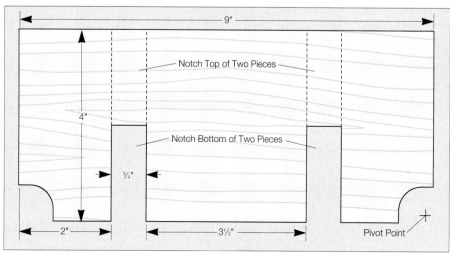

Overall View

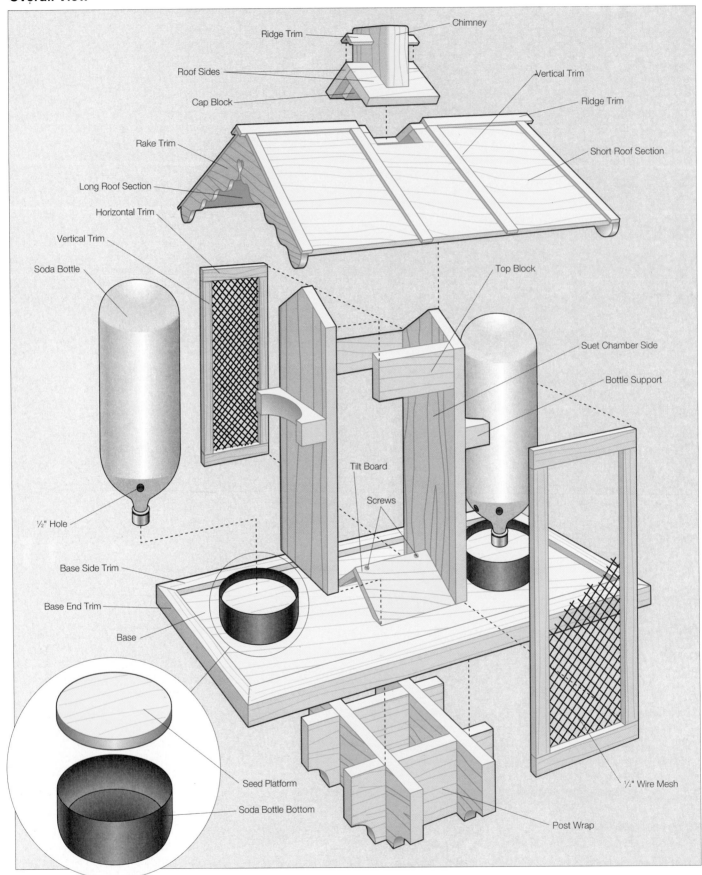

Chimney

Ridge Trim

Roof Sides

Cap Block

Vertical Trim

Ridge Trim

Rake Trim

Short Roof Section

Long Roof Section

Horizontal Trim

Vertical Trim

Top Block

Soda Bottle

Suet Chamber Side

Bottle Support

Tilt Board

½" Hole

Screws

Base Side Trim

Base End Trim

Base

¼" Wire Mesh

Seed Platform

Soda Bottle Bottom

Post Wrap

The post wrap is designed to hold your feeder on a 4x4 post. Cut the 4x9-inch pieces from one-by lumber. Lay out the notches and curves shown in Post-Wrap Layout. Use a compass to lay out the curves at a 1-inch radius and cut them with a coping saw or saber saw. Cut the sides of the notches with a handsaw or saber saw, then knock out the waste with a ¾-inch chisel cut across the bottom of each notch. Interlock the pieces.

Center the assembly on the bottom of the base, then secure it with 1⅝-inch screws through the top of the base. Use two screws into each of the four post-wrap pieces.

2 Make the Suet Chamber.

Cut the suet chamber sides and the tilt boards to the dimensions in the Cutting List. Cut two 45-degree angles to form a peak at the top of the chamber sides. Cut 45-degree bevels on the bottom of each tilt-board piece as shown in the Overall View, then screw the tilt boards together with two 1¼-inch screws.

To make the top blocks, cut a piece of ½-inch-thick plywood 2½ inches wide and about 12 inches long. (This is longer than you need for the blocks but the minimum length you can safely rip on the table saw.) Then cut the two 4-inch-long top blocks from the piece of stock.

Attach the sides of the suet chamber to the tilt boards with 1⅝-inch screws. Attach the tilt-board assembly, centered, to the base with four 2½-inch screws. Attach the chamber sides to the top blocks with two countersunk 1⅝-inch screws on each side.

Cut the wire mesh and the suet-chamber trim to the dimensions in the Cutting List. Attach the mesh to the sides of the suet chamber by nailing on the surrounding trim with brads.

Bottle-Support Layout

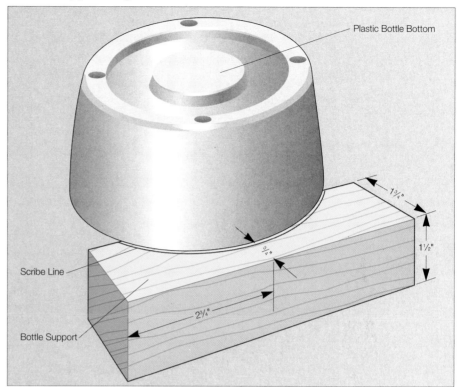

Plastic Bottle Bottom

Scribe Line

Bottle Support

1¾"

1½"

¾"

2¾"

3 Cut and Install the Bottle Supports.

Fill the 2-liter soda bottles with hot water. The heat from the water will soften the adhesive that holds the label and plastic bottom in place. Remove the bottoms from the bottles.

Cut the bottle supports to the dimensions in the Cutting List. Position the bottle bottom piece upside down on the stock and scribe the curve as shown in Bottle-Support Layout. Attach the cup hooks to the supports, then attach the supports to the sides of the suet chamber about 7 inches from the base with two 1⅝-inch-long screws.

4 Cut and Attach the Roof Parts.

Cut the two roof sections to the dimensions in the Cutting List. Cut the chimney notches centered in one long edge of each roof section. Note that the long roof piece gets a deeper notch than the short piece. Now lap the long roof section over the short one and fasten them with 1⅝-inch screws. Center the roof assembly over the base and attach it to the suet chamber with two 1⅝-inch screws in each side piece.

Cut the vertical and ridge roof trim pieces to the dimensions in the Cutting List. Fasten the trim to the roof with brads as shown in the Overall View. Be sure to lap the wide ridge trim over the narrow trim.

Use a coping saw or scroll saw to cut the gingerbread rake pieces from ¼-inch plywood as shown in Rake Pattern. The pattern shown is 50 percent of its actual size. To make it full-size, reproduce it on a photocopier set at 200 percent. Or you can use the grid to make a pattern of any size you want. Of course, you can create your own design instead, if you like. Cut the pattern out and use tape or contact adhesive to place it directly onto your stock. If you plan to make multiple copies of the feeder, glue the pattern to thicker paperboard. Cut out

Rake Pattern

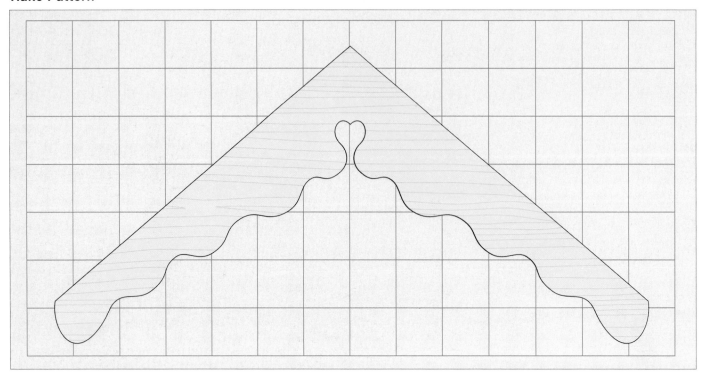

the paperboard pattern, then outline the pattern onto the wood. Attach the gingerbread trim with brads.

5 **Assemble the Chimney Cap.** Cut the chimney and chimney-cap sides, trim, and blocks to the dimensions in the Cutting List. Attach the sides to each other with glue and 1¼-inch screws, lapping the long piece over the short one.

Notch the chimney to fit over the cap, then round the edges that are not notched with a rasp and sandpaper. Center the chimney on the cap and attach it by driving a 1¼-inch screw up through the bottom of the cap.

Position the blocks under the cap so that the long block overlaps the short one. Secure the blocks with glue and one ¾-inch screw into each block. Fasten the ridge trim to the top of the cap with brads. Lap the wide piece over the narrow one.

6 **Make the Seed Platforms.** Measure and cut two 4¼-inch-diameter circles from one-by material to serve as seed platforms in the bottle bottoms. The circles should be beveled to fit snugly inside the bottoms. You can cut the circles using a band saw with the table tilted about 60 degrees. Or you can use a saber saw or coping saw, then clamp the workpiece and bevel the edges with a belt sander. Position the seed platforms in the bottle bottoms.

Drill two or three ½-inch holes just above the bottle necks. The holes will allow seed to fall onto the bottle-bottom assembly. As birds pull seed out of the holes, more will fall onto the base.

7 **Finish the Feeder.** Paint the project the color(s) of your choice.

Fill the suet chamber with suet, bread, or fruit, making sure the food is pushed against the wire mesh. Fill the soda bottles with birdseed and screw their caps on. Place the seed platforms on the base and turn the bottles upside down onto the platforms. Secure the bottles with rubber bands hooked over the cup hooks.

Bird Feeder/Robin's Roost

This platform bird feeder doubles as a protected—but open—nesting site for robins in the spring.

Birds have different needs at different times of the year. In the winter they spend most of their time foraging for food. In the spring, when food becomes more plentiful, their main attention shifts to finding a suitable spot to build a nest and start a family.

This project is designed to meet a bird's changing needs. During the winter, fill the platform with seed or use a mason jar as a seed holder. Fill the jar with seed, then turn it over onto wooden lifters (see Step 4 on page 66). Remove the seed in the spring and summer months, and your feeder becomes the perfect robin's roost. In fact, robins prefer building their nests in open roosts as compared with the best-built birdhouses! Just make sure the roost is out of the way of busy areas so you don't disturb the nesting birds.

CUTTING & MATERIALS LIST

Part	Quantity	Dimensions	Part	Quantity	Dimensions
Base	1	¾"x7¼"x7¼"	Base front trim	1	¾"x1½"x8¾"
Back	1	¾"x6¼"x12"	Shingles	10	⅛"x2½"x11¼"
Roof	2	¾"x5½"x10"	Roof-ridge trim	2	⅛"x¾"x11"
Ceiling piece	1	¾"x3½"x7½"	Deck screws		1¼" long
Gable trim	1	¼"x1½"x11"	Brads		1" long
Base bracket	1	¾"x2½"x3½"	Mason jar	1	
Side brackets	2	½"x2½"x3½"	Silicone sealant		
Mason-jar lifters	2	½"x½"x4"	Wood glue		
Base side trim	2	¾"x1½"x8"	Paint		

Difficulty Level:

Overall View

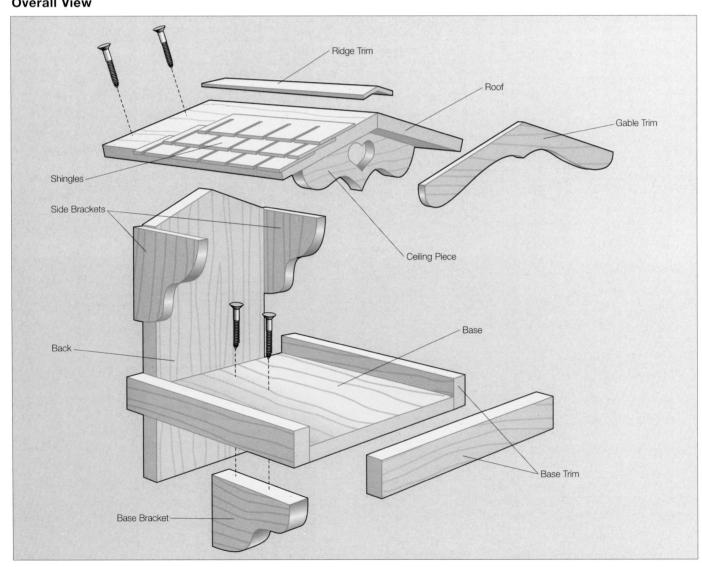

Ridge Trim

Roof

Gable Trim

Shingles

Side Brackets

Ceiling Piece

Back

Base

Base Trim

Base Bracket

Back Layout

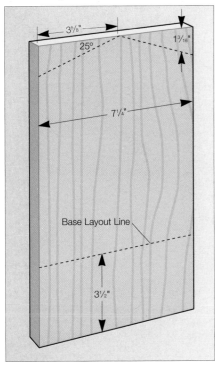

BUILDING THE FEEDER

1 Cut Out the Main Feeder Pieces. Cut the back, base, and roof pieces to the dimensions in the Cutting List. On a table saw, cut a 25-degree bevel on one long edge of each roof piece. Cut the roof pitch on the back piece as shown in Back Layout. Round all but the roof-pitch cuts with a ¼-inch roundover bit in a router or with a cabinet rasp and some sandpaper.

2 Cut the Pattern Pieces. Enlarge the ceiling-piece, gable-trim, and bracket patterns by photocopying them at 200 percent or use the grid to make your own patterns. Cut the patterns out and transfer them onto wood, then cut the pieces with a band saw or saber saw. Note that the base and side brackets use the same pattern but are different thicknesses. Make the heart-shaped cutout in the ceiling piece by drilling a starter hole and finishing the cutout with a coping saw or saber saw. Round the curved edges with a ¼-inch roundover bit or a rasp and sandpaper.

3 Assemble the Frame. Draw a horizontal reference line 3½ inches up from the bottom of the back. Place the bottom of the base along this line and attach the base with glue and countersunk screws through the back. Center the base bracket under the base and secure it with two countersunk screws, one through the base and one through the back.

Ceiling-Piece Pattern

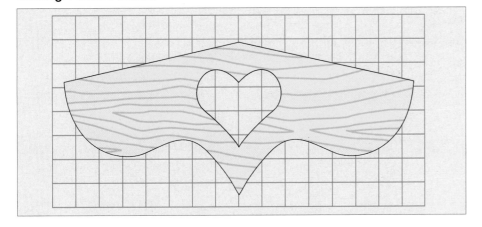

Bracket Pattern

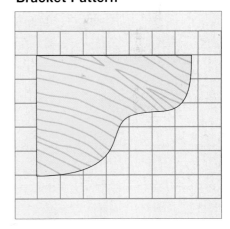

Gable-Trim Pattern

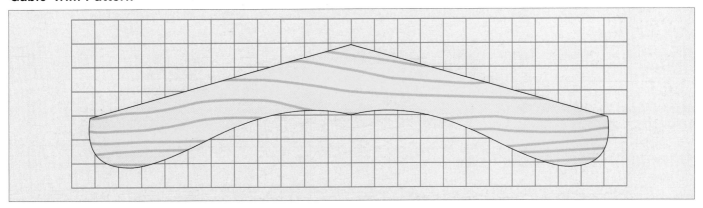

Cut the front and side base trim pieces to the dimensions in the Cutting List. Attach the pieces flush with the underside of the base using glue and countersunk screws. Glue wood plugs into the screw holes and sand the plugs flush.

4 **Install the Feeder Lifters.**
In the spring and summer, robins may use the roost as a nesting site. During the fall and winter, you can make the platform into a feeder by spreading seed every few days or installing a seed-filled mason jar upside down on lifters. To secure the mason jar, attach two $\frac{1}{2}$-inch cup hooks to the back, centered and at least 4 inches apart and 5 inches up from the base. You'll attach a rubber band to the cup hooks to hold the jar.

Measure and cut the mason jar lifters to $\frac{1}{2}$x$\frac{1}{2}$x4 inches. Notch the centers $\frac{1}{4}$x$\frac{3}{4}$ inch so that they overlap as shown in Jar-Lifter Layout. Cut the notches $\frac{1}{4}$ inch deep with a handsaw or coping saw, then knock out the waste with a $\frac{3}{4}$-inch chisel. Nail the lifter boards in place using wire brads.

To put the seed-filled mason jar in place, cover the top with a piece of cardboard. Turn the jar upside down on the lifters with the cardboard in place, then slip the cardboard out from under the jar.

5 **Attach the Roof and Trim.**
Install the roof pieces with countersunk wood screws through the top of the back piece. Drive two screws into each roof piece. Attach the side brackets with glue and brads.

Install the ceiling piece under the roof with glue and countersunk screws through the roof, then attach the gable trim flush with the top of the roof using glue and brads.

Jar-Lifter Layout

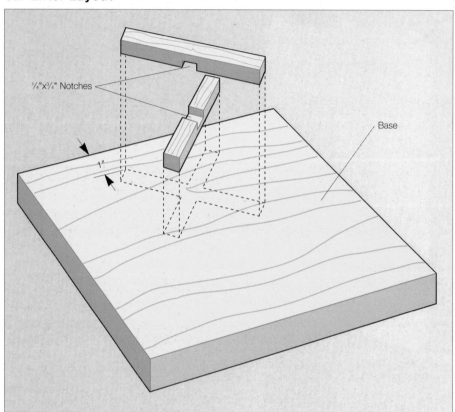

$\frac{1}{4}$"x$\frac{3}{4}$" Notches

1"

Base

Cutting the Shingle Blocks

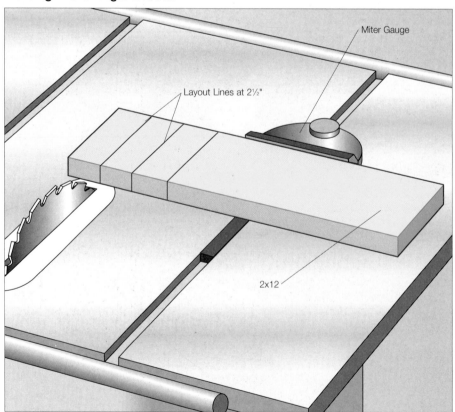

Miter Gauge

Layout Lines at 2½"

2x12

6 **Shingle the Roof.** First, cut three 2½-inch-wide pieces off a length of 2x12 as shown in Cutting the Shingle Blocks. You'll get about four shingle sections from each of the three pieces. Then cut 1-inch-deep kerfs spaced about 1 inch apart using a band saw or a table saw with the blade set 1 inch high as shown in Kerfing the Shingle Blocks. Slice the shingles to ⅛ inch thick with the band saw or table saw as shown in Slicing the Shingles. While you have the saw out, rip two ridge-trim pieces to the dimensions shown on the Cutting List from one-by stock.

Glue the shingles to the roof with silicone sealant, letting them overlap the eaves and ridges by about ½ inch. Lap the shingles by about 1 inch as you move up the roof. Attach the ridge trim with silicone.

7 **Finish the Feeder.** Paint the roost/feeder as desired and attach it to a post or tree with screws driven through the back.

Kerfing the Shingle Blocks

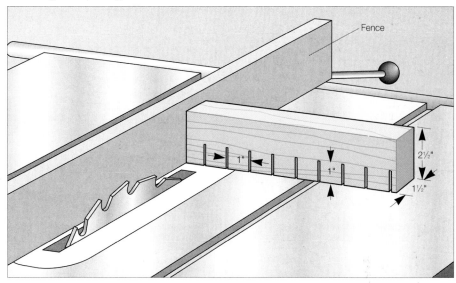

Slicing the Shingles

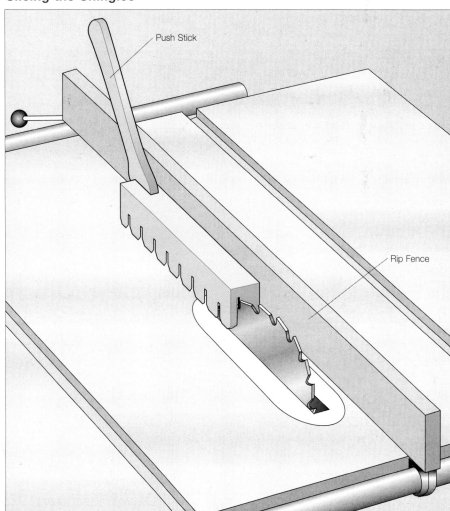

Tin~Can Seed Shoppe

A canvas awning protects the birdseed in this interpretation of a turn-of-the-century sweet shop.

The candy-cane colors of this feeder are reminiscent of an old-fashioned ice cream parlor. The Tin-Can Seed Shoppe advertises tasty goodies for all your feathered friends. By stocking each tin can with different kinds of seeds, you can try to satisfy even the pickiest eaters.

The Tin-Can Seed Shoppe makes use of empty coffee cans that might be on their way into the trash. The feeder is topped with canvas to keep the food dry and to protect birds from the weather. Try filling the coffee cans with sunflower seeds or raw peanuts and see if you can attract cardinals, goldfinches, grosbeaks, titmice, and woodpeckers. Birdseed mixtures with smaller seeds may attract cedar waxwings, sparrows, and a variety of songbirds. Watch out, though, because if you get a hungry bunch, the food will disappear right before your eyes. Make sure you have an extra supply of seeds on hand.

CUTTING & MATERIALS LIST

Part	Quantity	Dimensions
Base	1	½"x11½"x16"
Back	1	½"x11½"x16"
Can support	1	1½"x2½"x12"
Can risers	4	¼"x½"x6½"
Brackets	2	¾"x5½"x5½"
Side trim	2	⅝"x1"x6⅛"
Front trim	1	⅝"x1"x17"
Posts	2	1"x1"x9"
Crosspiece	1	1"x1"x12½"
Front canvas hanger	1	¼"x½"x14½"

Part	Quantity	Dimensions
Back canvas hanger	1	½"x½"x16"
Canvas awning	1	13"x17"
Cup holders	3	¾" diameter
Coffee cans	2	
Deck screws		1¼" long
Brads		1" long
Rubber bands	2	large
Paint		
Glue		

Difficulty Level:

Overall View

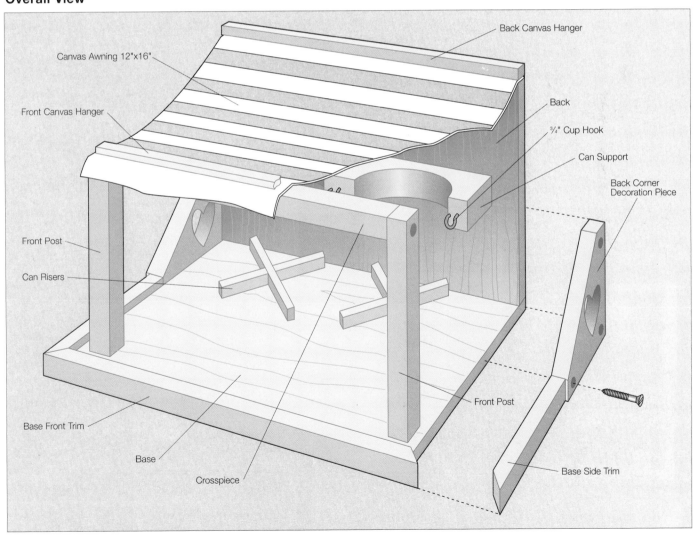

Back Canvas Hanger

Canvas Awning 12"x16"

Front Canvas Hanger

Back

¾" Cup Hook

Can Support

Back Corner Decoration Piece

Front Post

Can Risers

Front Post

Base Front Trim

Base

Crosspiece

Base Side Trim

BUILDING THE FEEDER

1 Assemble the Base, Back, and Can Support. Cut the base, back, and can support board to the dimensions in the Cutting List. Join the base and back pieces with glue and three screws driven up through the base and into the back.

Position the two coffee cans on the can support board 1 inch from each side and 1¼ inches from the back as shown in Can Support and Risers Layout. Scribe around the bottom of the cans. Cut to these lines with a coping saw or saber saw.

Draw a line across the back about 4¼ inches up from the bottom. Align the bottom of the can support with this line and attach it with three screws through the back. Attach the three cup holders to the support board as shown in Can Support and Risers Layout.

Cut the can risers to the dimensions in the Cutting List. Notch the risers to overlap each other as shown in the drawing. Nail the risers in place with brads.

After filling the tin cans with seed, place a piece of cardboard over the top, tip the can over, place the covered can on the risers, then remove the cardboard. Some seed will fall out. More seed with fall out as the birds eat what's on the platform.

2 Make the Brackets. Cut the brackets as shown in Bracket Layout. The heart-shaped cutouts are, of course, optional. To make them, use a spade bit to drill two side-by-side 1-inch-diameter holes. Lay out the rest of the heart shape freehand, then finish the cut with a coping saw or saber saw. On the outside faces of the brackets, round-over the inside edges of the heart with a ¼-inch roundover bit in a router, or simply smooth the edges with sandpaper. Attach the pieces to both the base and the back using 1¼-inch screws and glue.

3 Install the Front and Side Trim. Cut the side and back trim pieces to the dimensions in the Cutting List, mitering the front corners. Smooth the long edges of the trim with a rasp and sandpaper or the ¼-inch roundover bit. Attach the trim to the base with glue and brads.

4 Attach the Posts and Crosspiece. Cut the posts and the crosspiece to the dimensions in the Cutting List. Position the posts on the base as shown in Can Support and Risers Layout. Attach each post with a countersunk screw through the base. Attach the crosspiece to the posts with a screw in a counterbored hole through the posts. Then attach the assembly to the base with one countersunk screw into each post.

5 Finish the Feeder. Hem the canvas ½ inch on all four sides, to a finished dimension of 12x16 inches. Measure and cut the front and back canvas hangers. Sandwich the canvas between the back canvas hanger and the back piece. Tack brads through the hanger and canvas and into the back piece. Leave a little slack in the awning so that if it shrinks after the first rainstorm, it won't pull your posts out of position. Sandwich the canvas between the front canvas hanger and the crosspiece and front posts. Tack the front canvas hanger in place with brads.

Paint and decorate the finished feeder as desired.

Can Support and Risers Layout

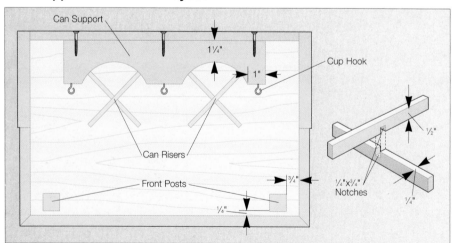

Bracket Layout

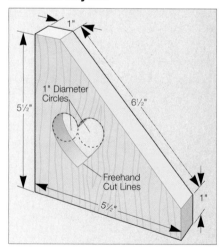

Multilevel Seed Silo

Made from scraps of large-diameter plastic drainpipe, this practical feeder holds a bounty of birdseed and demands minimal attention to upkeep.

This feeder has chambers made of 6-inch-diameter polyvinyl chloride (PVC) pipe, which is available at any home center or plumbing store. The chambers hold plenty of seeds, a big advantage when you discover how hungry birds can get during the winter. The PVC also makes the feeder easy to construct, as long as you have a band saw or saber saw.

If you like, attach baffles to the feeder's hanging wires or chains to try to keep the squirrels out. If you don't mind feeding the neighborhood squirrels along with birds, try putting the feeder on the ground instead of hanging it. You'll probably find that the bird species it attracts on the ground are different from those that come when the feeder is hung. A feeder placed on the ground and filled with inexpensive cracked corn or mixed seed will attract large groups of primarily ground-feeding birds like doves, juncos, blackbirds, and sparrows.

CUTTING & MATERIALS LIST

Part	Quantity	Dimensions	Part	Quantity	Dimensions
Base feed platform	1	¾"x14" diameter	Lid base	1	¾"x6" diameter
Base lip	1	¾"x14" diameter with 13" hole	First-tier lid	1	¾"x10" diameter
Second-level feed platform	1	¾"x12" diameter with 3" hole	Second-tier lid	1	¾"x7" diameter
Second-level lip	1	¾"x12" diameter with 11" hole	Lid top	1	¾"x4" diameter
Second-level support disks	2	¾"x6" diameter with 3" hole	Screw eyes	2	¾" diameter
Base support disk	1	¾"x6" diameter	Deck screws		1" long
PVC bottom feed chamber	1	6" diameter x9"	Deck screws		1¼" long
PVC top feed chamber	1	6" diameter x6"	Wood plugs		Sized to match countersink
			Exterior caulk		
			Wire or chain		
			Paint		

Difficulty Level: 🔨 🔨

BUILDING THE FEEDER

1 Make the Feed Platforms. Use a compass to lay out the 14-inch-diameter base feed platform on a piece of ¾-inch plywood. Cut the circle out with a band saw or saber saw. For the base lip, use the compass to lay out another 14-inch-diameter circle. Then adjust the compass for a 13-inch circle and draw another circle from the same pivot point as the first. Cut the lines to make the lip. Round-over the top edges of the lip with a router set in a router table and equipped with a ¼-inch roundover bit. If you don't have a router table, don't try to do this with a hand-held router; there isn't enough support for the router base to do it safely. Instead, round the edges with a rasp or file and sandpaper. Glue and clamp the base lip to the base feed platform.

Set the compass to a 12-inch diameter for the second-level feed platform and outside circumference of the lip, then set it for an 11-inch diameter for the inside circumference of the lip. After you cut the base out, lay out a 3-inch-diameter circle in the middle. Drill a starter hole in the circle adjacent to the layout line and complete the cut with a coping saw or saber saw.

2 Make the Feed Chambers. Using a hacksaw, cut 6-inch-diameter PVC pipe to the dimensions in the Cutting List to make two feeding chambers. Drill three equally spaced ¾-inch diameter holes located ¾ inch from the bottom of each chamber as shown in the Overall View. Sand the edges of the PVC smooth.

3 Make the Support Disks and Lid Base. As shown in the Overall View, the feed chambers are attached to the feed platforms with three 6-inch-diameter plywood or solid-wood disks. The lid base is made of the same materials with the same dimensions. Use the inside diameter of your feed chambers to scribe the diameters of the support disks and lid base, then cut them out with a saber saw. Cut a 3-inch-diameter hole in two of the disks as you did for the second-level feed platform.

4 Assemble the Feeder. Attach the base support disk (the disk without a hole) to the center of the base feed platform with glue and one countersunk 1¼-inch screw.

Put the bottom chamber in position over the base support disk. Predrill and counterbore four evenly spaced holes through the bottom chamber into the base support disk. Use a ⅜-inch-diameter bit for the counterbores. Drive 1-inch-long screws into the holes.

Attach one support disk to the top of the second-level feed platform and one to the bottom. Make sure the 3-inch holes are aligned, then attach the disks with glue and countersunk 1¼-inch wood screws. Attach this assembly to the top and bottom feed chambers with four evenly spaced 1-inch screws.

5 Make the Lid. Cut the lid top, second-tier lid, and first-tier lid to the dimensions in the Cutting List. Round the top and bot-

Overall View

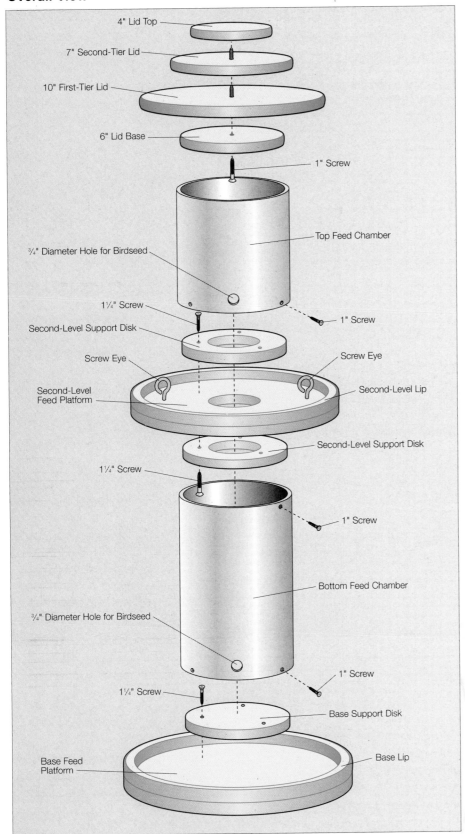

- 4" Lid Top
- 7" Second-Tier Lid
- 10" First-Tier Lid
- 6" Lid Base
- 1" Screw
- ¾" Diameter Hole for Birdseed
- Top Feed Chamber
- 1¼" Screw
- Second-Level Support Disk
- 1" Screw
- Screw Eye
- Screw Eye
- Second-Level Feed Platform
- Second-Level Lip
- Second-Level Support Disk
- 1¼" Screw
- Bottom Feed Chamber
- 1" Screw
- ¾" Diameter Hole for Birdseed
- 1" Screw
- 1¼" Screw
- Base Support Disk
- Base Feed Platform
- Base Lip

tom edges of the first tier, and the top edges of the top and second tier with a ¼-inch roundover bit in the router. If you don't have a router, use a rasp or file and sandpaper.

Attach the second tier to the top with glue and one countersunk 1¼-inch screw. Attach the first tier to the second tier the same way, then attach the lid base you cut earlier to the first tier, also the same way. Offset the screws a bit so they don't interfere with each other.

6 Finish the Project. Paint the feeder the color(s) of your choice. Use spray paint to avoid brush marks on the pipe. If you intend to hang the feeder, fasten two screw eyes to the outer edges of the second-level feed platform and attach chain or wire to the screw eyes. Fill the feeder with birdseed and attach the lid assembly.

Squirrel Feeder

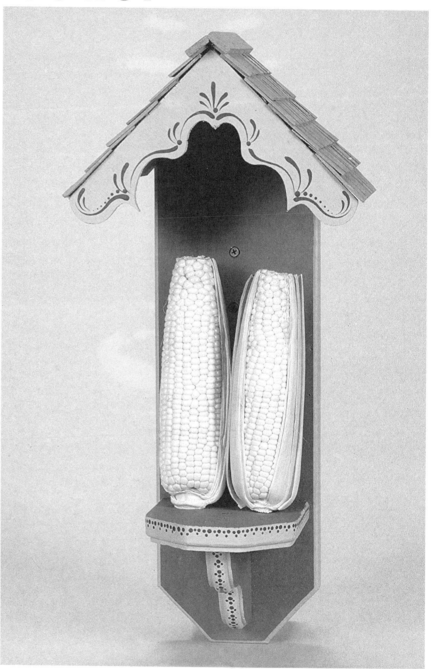

If you keep the squirrels satisfied at their own feeder, they may not raid neighboring bird feeders. Or so goes the theory. You can test that theory with this handsome design.

Squirrels can be a constant nuisance when you set out to feed birds. The nut- and seed-loving animals like free food just as much as birds do, and if given the chance, will scare the birds away from their feeder. A lot of gadgets claim that they'll keep your feeder "squirrel-free," and they might—but only for a short while. Eventually, the little furry bandits will outsmart the gadget.

Fortunately, most squirrels are not above accepting a simple bribe. If you offer them easy access to food they like in this Squirrel Feeder, you might dissuade them from pilfering a harder-to-get-at bird feeder. Stick dried corn-on-the-cob, sunflower heads, or other food on the screws, and find out what the squirrels like. For a change, watch and see whether the birds try to steal the squirrels' food.

CUTTING & MATERIALS LIST

Part	Quantity	Dimensions	Part	Quantity	Dimensions
Back	1	¾"x5½"x18"	Ridge trim	1	¼"x¾"x6¼"
Long roof piece	1	¾"x5½"x 5¾"	Shingles	12	⅛"x2"x7¼"
Short roof piece	1	¾"x5½"x5"	Deck screws		1¼" long
Feed platform	1	¾"x5"x5½"	Deck screws		2" long
Bracket	1	¾" thick, cut to shape	Brads		¾" long
Gable trim	1	¼" thick, cut to shape	Silicone sealant		
			Glue		
Ridge trim	1	¼"x1"x6¼"	Paint		

Difficulty Level:

Overall View

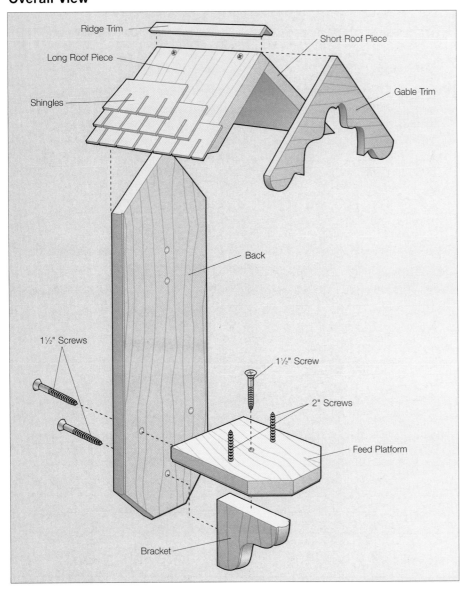

Ridge Trim
Long Roof Piece
Shingles
Short Roof Piece
Gable Trim
Back
1½" Screws
1½" Screw
2" Screws
Feed Platform
Bracket

BUILDING THE FEEDER

1 Cut the Major Frame Pieces. From a 1x6, measure and cut the back, long roof, short roof, and feed platform to the dimensions in the Cutting List. Cut a 45-degree bevel on a long end of each roof piece.

Use a protractor or combination square to lay out the 45-degree cuts at the top and bottom of the back piece and on the feed platform as shown in Back Layout and Feed Platform Layout. Make these cuts.

2 Cut the Patterned Pieces. Enlarge the Bracket Pattern and Gable Trim Pattern by reproducing them on a photocopy machine set at 200 percent. You can also use the grid to make your own patterns if you can't get access to an enlarging photocopier. Cut out the patterns. Tape the gable trim pattern to a piece of ¼-inch-thick plywood. Tape the bracket pattern to a piece of one-by stock. Cut out the pieces with a coping saw or saber saw.

3 Rout the Decorative Edges. You'll cut a decorative

Back Layout

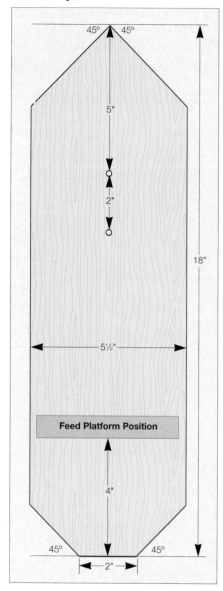

Bracket Pattern

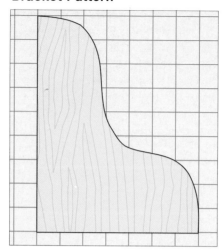

Gable Trim Pattern

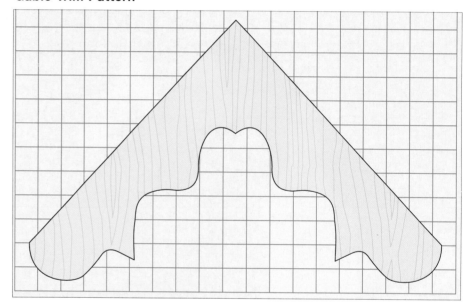

edge into the bottom and sides (but not the top) of the back piece, the front and side bottom edges of the feed platform, and both front edges of the bracket as shown in the Overall View.

To make the decorative edges, put a ⅛-inch roundover bit in a router. The pieces are small, so set the router in a router table. Set the bit to create a ⅛-inch-deep lip as shown in Routing the Decorative Edge.

If you don't have a router table, round the edges gently with a rasp

Feed Platform Layout

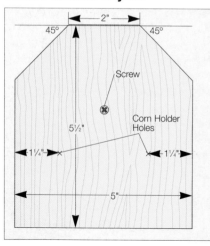

Routing the Decorative Edge

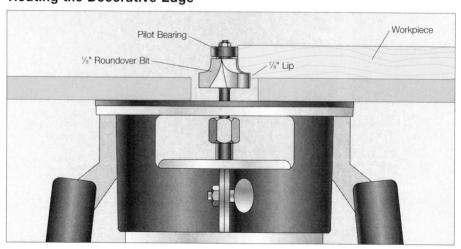

and sandpaper. You'll still have a beautiful feeder.

4 **Assemble the Feeder.** Lap the long roof piece over the short one and attach them with two countersunk 1¼-inch screws as shown in the Overall View. Attach the roof assembly to the back with two countersunk 1¼-inch screws through each roof piece.

Draw a reference line across the back piece, 4 inches from the bottom as shown in Back Layout. Align the bottom of the feeder platform with this line and attach it with two countersunk 1¼-inch screws through the back of the feeder.

Center the bracket you cut in Step 2 under the feed platform and secure it with one countersunk 1¼-inch screw through the platform and one through the back. Attach the gable trim to the front of the roof with glue and brads.

5 **Make the Shingles.** First, cut three 2½-inch-wide pieces off a length of 2x8 as shown in Cutting the Shingle Blocks. Then cut 1-inch-deep kerfs spaced about 1 inch apart using a band saw or a table saw with the blade set 1 inch high as shown in Kerfing the Shingle

Blocks. Now slice the shingles to ⅛ inch thick with the band saw or table saw as shown in Slicing the Shingles. You'll get about four shingle courses from each of the three pieces. Cut the shingles to fit the roof with an overhang of about ½ inch at the front gable and eaves. Attach the shingles with dabs of silicone sealant, overlapping them by about 1 inch as you work your way up the roof.

Cut the roof ridge trim to the dimensions in the Cutting List. Position the trim with the wider piece overlapping the narrower piece and attach it with glue and brads.

6 **Finish the Feeder.** Counterbore two holes in the back, positioning them as shown in the Overall View. Drive two 2-inch screws up through the bottom of the feed platform to protrude through the top of the platform. Use these screws for attaching food.

Paint the project the color(s) of your choice. Attach the feeder to a tree with 2-inch screws through the holes in the back. "Screw" the corn or other food in place, and your feeder is open for business.

Cutting the Shingle Blocks

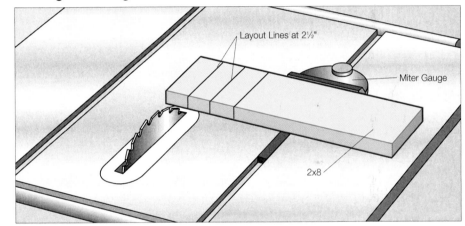

Kerfing the Shingle Blocks

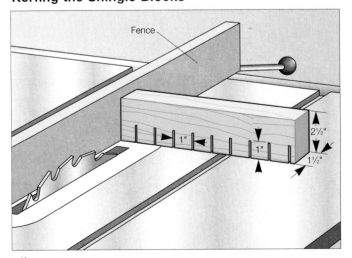

Slicing the Shingles

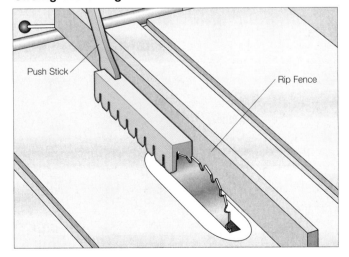

Seed Bell Shelter

Intricately cut trim and wooden roof shingles add style to an ordinary seed bell and keep it dry in inclement weather.

Here's a humdinger of a project both you and your feathered friends will enjoy. You hang a standard bell-shaped seed ball, found at most grocery and pet-supply stores, from the feeder. The bells come in various sizes, and this feeder will accommodate all of them. All you have to do is attach the bell to the cup hook and wait for the birds to find the treasure.

Cutting & Materials List

Part	Quantity	Dimensions
Long roof section	1	¾"x7¼"x7"
Short roof section	1	¾"x6½"x7"
Gable trim	2	¾" thick, cut to shape
Peak trim	1	¾" thick, cut to shape
Ceiling board	1	1"x1¼"x7"
Ridge board	1	1"x1½"x8½"
Shingles	12	⅛"x2½"x9¼"

Part	Quantity	Dimensions
Cup hook	1	1" diameter
Screw eye	1	½" diameter
Deck screws		1¼" long
Deck screws		1½" long
Wood plugs		Sized to fit the countersink
Glue		
Silicone		
Paint		

Difficulty Level:

Overall View

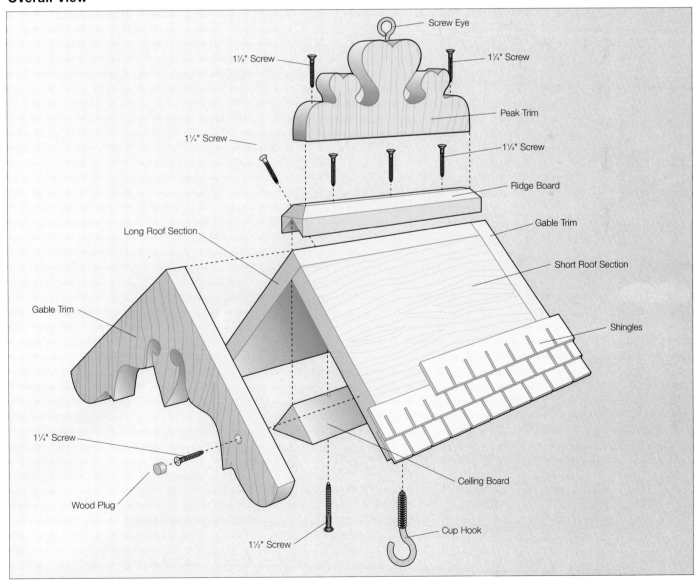

Screw Eye

1¼" Screw

1¼" Screw

Peak Trim

1¼" Screw

1¼" Screw

Ridge Board

Gable Trim

Long Roof Section

Short Roof Section

Gable Trim

Shingles

1¼" Screw

Wood Plug

Ceiling Board

1½" Screw

Cup Hook

BUILDING THE FEEDER

1 **Assemble the Roof.** Cut the long and short roof sections from 1x8s to the dimensions in the Cutting List. Attach the long piece along one edge of the short one with glue and two countersunk 1¼-inch screws.

2 **Attach the Ridge and Ceiling Boards.** Rip the ridge board from two-by material 1 inch thick and 8½ inches long. Chamfer the board along the top and notch it at the bottom to fit on

Shaping the Ridge Board

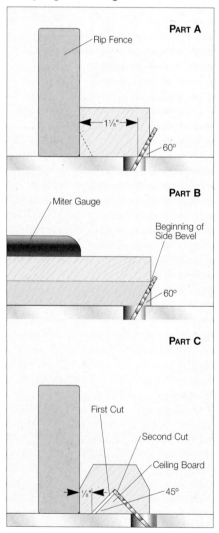

the roof. You can make the chamfers and notch in three table-saw operations as shown in Shaping the Ridge Board. Be sure to use a push stick for the ripping operations.

First, set the table-saw height to ⅞ inch, with the blade tilted at 60 degrees. Set the rip fence 1⅛ inches from the blade, as shown in Part A of Shaping the Ridge Board. Note that on many table saws the blade tilts to the right when viewed from the operator's side. If you have this kind of saw, put the fence to the left of the blade as shown. Run both sides of one face over the blade to chamfer the sides. To chamfer the ends of the ridge board, remove the rip fence and use the miter gauge set at 90 degrees, as shown in Part B of Shaping the Ridge Board.

To make the notch, leave the blade height at ⅞ inch. Change the blade tilt to 45 degrees, as shown in Part C of Shaping the Ridge Board. Set the rip fence to ⅛ inch from the blade, as shown. Run the piece through twice to make the notch.

As you near the end of the second cut, place a sacrificial piece of stock

against the operator's end of the ridge board to prevent the triangular piece from shooting back at you when it's cut free. This sacrificial piece should be at least ¾x1½ x12 inches. Reduce the triangular cutoff to 7 inches long, and you'll have the ceiling board.

Attach the ceiling board to the underside of the roof with glue and two countersunk 1½-inch screws as shown in the Overall View. Then attach the ridge board with glue and three countersunk 1¼-inch screws.

3 **Attach the Gable and Peak Trim.** Enlarge the Gable Trim Pattern and Peak Trim Pattern by reproducing them on a photocopy machine set at 200 percent. Copy the gable trim twice. If you don't have access to an enlarging photocopier, use the grid to create your own patterns. Cut out the three patterns and tape them on one-by lumber. Following the patterns, cut out the pieces with a coping saw, saber saw, or scroll saw.

Attach the peak trim to the ridge board with two countersunk 1¼-inch screws, as shown in the Overall View. Attach each gable trim piece to the

Gable Trim Pattern

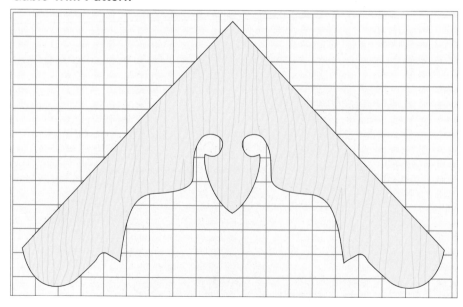

roof with glue and two countersunk 1¼-inch screws, as shown. Glue wood plugs into the counterbored holes and sand the plugs flush.

4 **Shingle the Roof.** Begin by cutting three 2½-inch-wide pieces off a length of 2x10, as shown in Cutting the Shingle Blocks. You'll get about four shingle sections from each of the three pieces. Then cut 1-inch-deep kerfs spaced about 1 inch apart. Make the cuts with a band saw or a table saw with the blade set 1 inch high as shown in Kerfing the Shingle Blocks. Slice the shingles to ⅛ inch thick on the band saw or table saw as shown in Slicing the Shingles. Now attach the shingles to the roof course by course with silicone, being careful to stagger the joints between the shingles as you go up the roof. Leave a ¼-inch overhang on the gable ends and ½ inch at the eaves; overlap the shingle rows by 1 inch.

5 **Finish the Feeder.** Paint the project the color(s) of your choice. Attach the cup hook to the center of the ceiling and the screw eye to the top of the peak trim.

Peak Trim Pattern

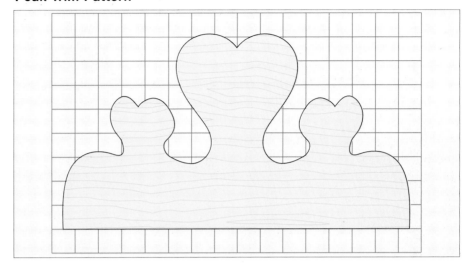

Cutting the Shingle Blocks

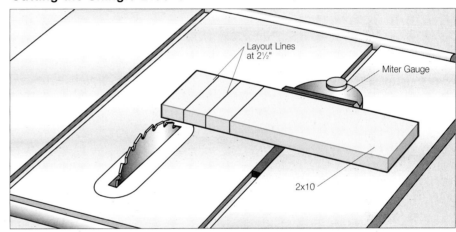

Kerfing the Shingle Blocks

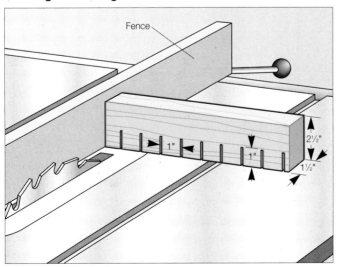

Slicing the Shingles

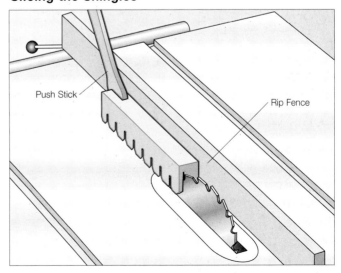

Pig Bird Feeder

Pigs are a popular motif in folk art, and this one should be popular with the backyard birds because it serves as the perfect seed bank.

The Pig Bird Feeder brings the farm to you. Because the pig is hollow, you can fill it with an abundance of seeds. You'll spend more time watching the birds and less time refilling the feeder, and the birds will be happy because they'll have lots of food.

The pig is a lamination of 2x10s hollowed out and covered with shaped 1x12 outer body parts. It sits on an octagon-shaped platform made from ½-inch plywood. Seeds fall out the bottom opening of the pig onto the plat-

form as birds consume them. The heart cutout is made into a window covered with acrylic glazing. The clear plastic lets you see the seed level so you know when it's time to refill the feeder.

Spend some time to do a careful paint job, and this project will keep the neighbors talking. With the post wraps, you can perch the feeder on top of any 4x4 post. Put it on a fence or deck railing, or place it in your favorite spot for bird-watching.

CUTTING & MATERIALS LIST

Part	Quantity	Dimensions
Base	1	½"x20"x20"
Base trim	8	¾"x1"x8¼"
Post wraps	4	¾"x5½"x16"
Pig outer body	2	¾"x11¼"x15½", cut to shape
Inner chamber	2	1½"x9¼"x16½", cut to shape
Pig's tail	1	¾"x1½"x2", cut to shape
Hat top	1	¾"x2½" diameter
Hat rim	1	⅜"x4" diameter
Hat insert	1	¾"x1¾" diameter

Part	Quantity	Dimensions
Acrylic glazing	1	⅛"x4" square
Deck screws		1" long
Deck screws		1⅝" long
Deck screw		1¾" long
Deck screws		1¼" long
Brass wood screws		½" long
Wood plugs		Sized to fit countersink
Glue		
Paint		

Difficulty Level:

Overall View

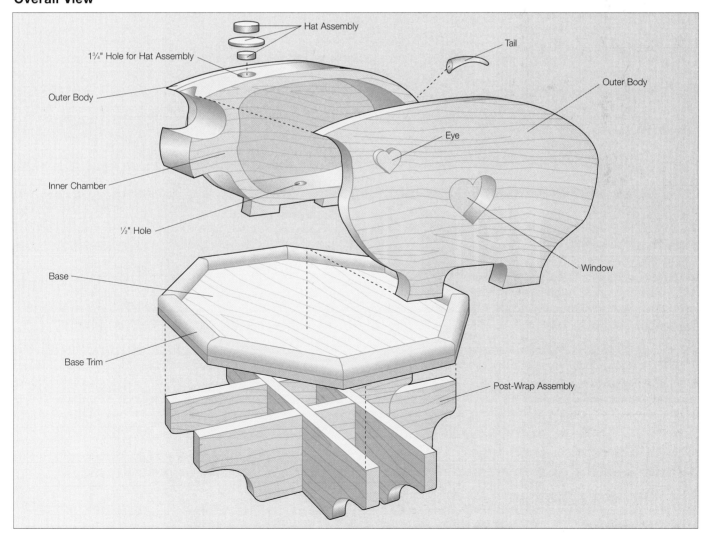

BUILDING THE FEEDER

1 Make the Base. Cut a piece of ½-inch plywood for the octagon base to the dimensions in the Cutting List. Then use a protractor or combination square to lay out the octagon's 45-degree angles, as shown in Base Layout. Make the cuts with a circular saw or saber saw.

Cut the base trim pieces to the dimensions in the Cutting List, with 67½-degree miters on each end. Attach the trim to the base with glue and two countersunk 1-inch screws through each trim piece into the base. Round-over the outside edges of the trim with a ¼-inch roundover bit in a router or with a rasp and sandpaper. Fill the holes with wood plugs and sand all the edges of the base.

2 Make the Post Wrap. The post wrap is designed to hold the feeder on a 4x4 post. Cut four 16-inch 1x6s. Lay out the notches and curves as shown in Post-Wrap Layout. Use a compass to lay out the 3-inch radius for the curves, then cut them out with a coping saw or saber saw. Round the curved edges of the post wrap with a ¼-inch roundover bit in the router or with a rasp and sandpaper. Cut the sides of the notches with a handsaw or saber saw, then knock out the waste with a ¾-inch chisel cut across the bottom of each notch. Interlock the pieces.

Center the assembly on the bottom of the base and secure it with 1⅝-inch deck screws through the base. Use two screws into each of the four post-wrap pieces.

3 Cut Out the Patterns. Enlarge the Pig Pattern by reproducing it on a photocopy

Base Layout

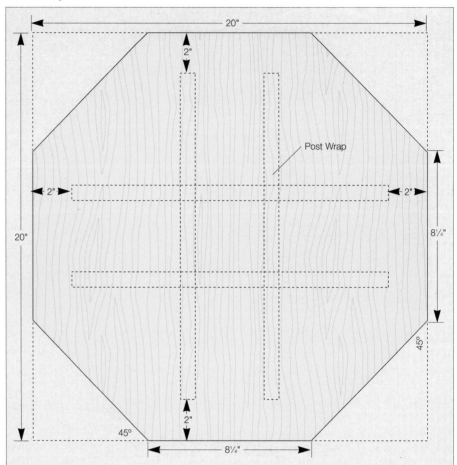

Post-Wrap Layout

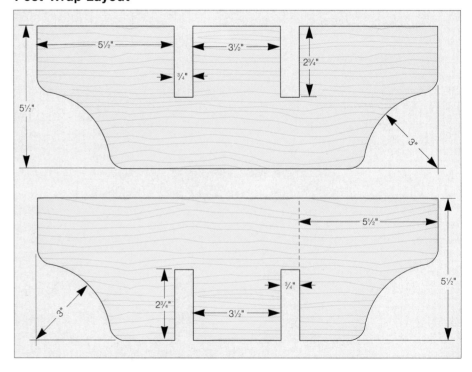

Pig Pattern

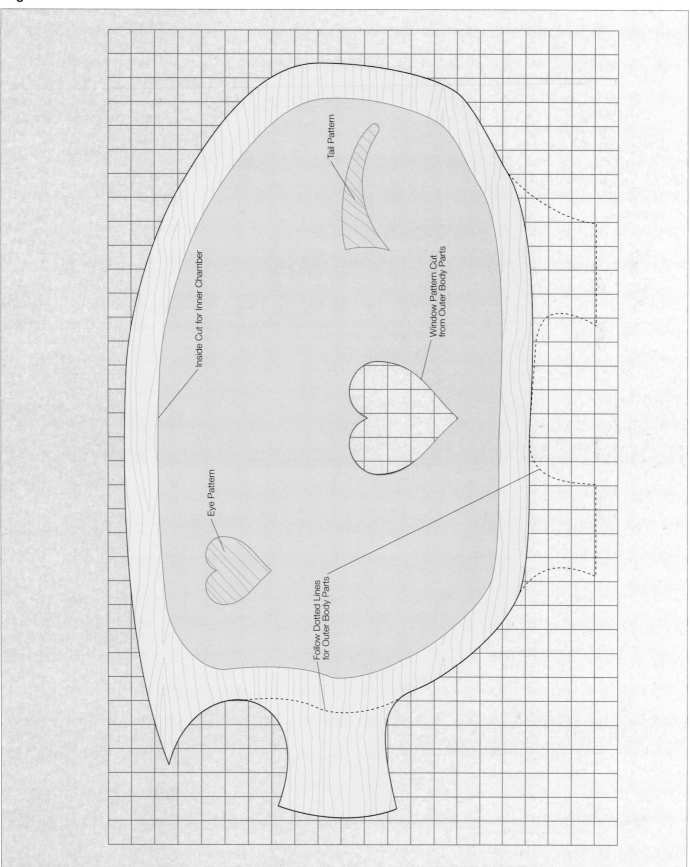

Tail Pattern

Inside Cut for Inner Chamber

Window Pattern Cut
from Outer Body Parts

Eye Pattern

Follow Dotted Lines
for Outer Body Parts

machine set at 200 percent. You can also use the grid to make your own pattern if you don't have access to an enlarging photocopier. Make two copies of the pattern. One of the copies will be for the outer body. When cutting the outer body pattern, follow the dotted lines to include the legs but not the nose. The other pattern will be for the inner chamber, as well as the tail and the heart-shaped eye and window. Cut out the inner chamber pattern to include the nose but not the legs. The cutout piece for the hollow inner chamber contains the patterns for the eye, window, and tail. Cut out these patterns.

4 Make the Outer Body. Cut two pieces of 1x12 15½ inches long. Tack the two pieces of wood together with a couple of brads. Tape the outer body pattern to the stacked wood. Cut out both outer bodies at the same time with a band saw, coping saw, saber saw, or scroll saw. While the pieces are still tacked together, sand the edges smooth and uniform.

5 Make the Inner Chamber. The inner chamber consists of two pieces of 2x10 laminated to form a 3-inch-thick piece. Cut these pieces to the dimensions in the Cutting List. If you have a band saw, glue the two pieces together now, tape the remaining pattern onto the sandwich, and cut out the pattern. With the band saw, enter the inner cut near the tail as shown in Pig Pattern.

If you try to use a saber saw, this method won't work well because the blade will wander in the 3-inch-deep cut. You'll have to cut the pieces individually. Once you've cut out the

body, drill a hole to start the inner cut. When you've finished cutting that piece, use it as a pattern for the other piece. When both pieces are cut, glue and clamp them together.

Trace the tail pattern onto one-by material and cut it out. Attach the tail to the inner chamber using glue and a 1¼ inch screw in a predrilled hole. Carefully shape the tail with a rasp and sandpaper to make it more realistic.

6 Make the Heart Cutout. As shown in the Overall View, the pig has a heart-shaped plastic window in one side so you can see when seed is running low. Trace the window pattern onto one outer body piece, positioning it as shown. The shape and exact size and position of the heart isn't important; in fact you could make a simple square window, if you like. Drill a hole and cut out the shape with a saber saw. Smooth the cut with a file.

Put a ⅜-inch rabbeting bit in a router and set the cutting depth to ⅛ inch. Run the bit around the heart to create a lipped outer heart. Tape a piece of cardboard over the hole. Plunge a matte knife into the cardboard, and guiding the knife along the inside of the outer heart shape, cut out a pattern. Tape this cardboard pattern to a piece of acrylic glazing and cut out the heart shape with a band saw, coping saw, or saber saw. Test-fit the window. If it's too tight, sand the edges. When the window fits, put it in place and drill and counterbore holes for two No. 4x½-inch flathead brass wood screws to hold the plastic in place.

7 Assemble the Pig. Place the inner chamber between

the outer body parts and clamp them together. Drill four countersunk holes through the outer body and into the inner chamber. Secure with glue and four 1¼-inch-long screws on each side.

Fill the countersunk holes with wood plugs and sand them smooth. Round the outer edges with a ¼-inch round-over bit in the router or with a rasp and sandpaper.

The shape of the rounded notch between the ears needn't be exact. Just lay it out freehand on top and cut it out with a saber saw.

8 Assemble the Hat, Dispenser, and Eye. Drill a 1¾-inch hole in the top of the pig body assembly as shown in the Overall View. This hole serves as an opening to pour seed. The hat serves as the lid. Drill a ½-inch hole in the bottom, centered between the four legs. This hole will dispense seed from the bottom of the pig onto the feeder base.

Use a compass to lay out the hat top, hat rim, and hat insert according to the dimensions in the Cutting List. Glue and screw the pieces together using a countersunk 1¾-inch screw. Round the top edges of the hat with a ¼-inch roundover bit on a router table or with a rasp and sandpaper.

Use the eye pattern to make two eyes from ¼-inch plywood. Glue the eyes in place.

9 Finish the Feeder. Paint the feeder to suit your taste. Fit the base over a 4x4 post. Set the pig on the base and fill it with seed.

Thistle Seed Dispenser

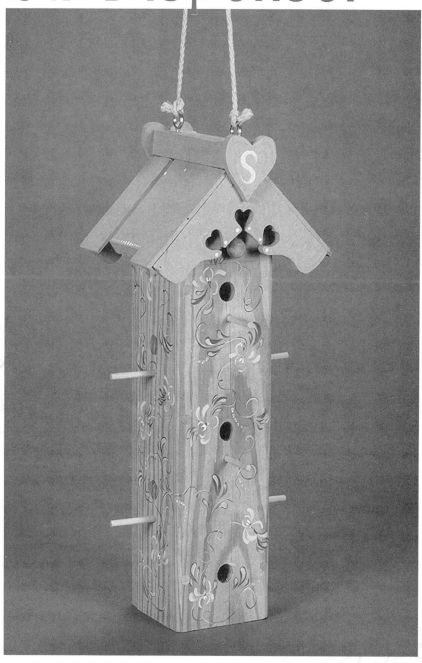

If you've ever tried to feed tiny thistle seed to birds, you know how difficult it is to dispense the seed without spilling it on the ground and wasting it. This clever design solves the problem elegantly.

Thistle seed is a delicacy that will attract chickadees, goldfinches, pine siskin, and other small birds. But there is a drawback to thistle. The seeds are so tiny that most bird feeders can't contain them properly and they end up pouring out onto the ground. To eliminate this problem, the Thistle Seed Dispenser is lined with a fine wire mesh, or screen, that holds the seeds without spilling them. Little birds can pluck the seeds one at a time from the minute screen openings. The screen also discourages bigger birds and squirrels who would otherwise intimidate the smaller birds.

Another practical feature is the "keyed-in" roof. Two dowel-and-ball "keys" tightly lock the roof onto the dispenser's feed chamber. Pull out the key, and the roof comes off the feed chamber for easy refilling.

CUTTING & MATERIALS LIST

Part	Quantity	Dimensions	Part	Quantity	Dimensions
Front and back	2	¾"x4½"x17"	Wire mesh (front & back)	2	2"x12"
Sides	2	¾"x3"x14¼"	Wire mesh (sides)	2	2"x8"
Long floor cleats	2	¼"x½"x3"	Wood balls	2	¾" diameter
Short floor cleats	2	¼"x½"x2½"	Staples		¼" long
Floor	1	¼"x3"x3"	Deck screws		1¼" long
Long roof piece	1	¾"x5¼"x5½"	Deck screws		1⅝" long
Short roof piece	1	¾"x4½"x5½"	Brads		½" long
Feed chamber hangers	2	¾"x2½"x3"	Brads		¾" long
Ridge board	1	1"x1½"x6½"	Wood plugs		Sized to fit countersink
Gable trim	2	⅜" thick (cut to shape)	Screw eyes	2	⅝" diameter
Heart trim	2	⅜" thick (cut to shape)	Wire or chain		
Roof trim	4	⅛"x1½"x5"	Paint, stain, or water sealer		
Wood dowels	12	¼" diameter x2½"			

Difficulty Level:

Feed Chamber Layout

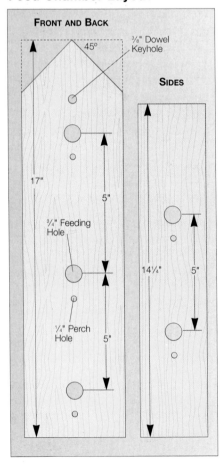

FRONT AND BACK

45°

⅜" Dowel Keyhole

SIDES

17"

5"

¾" Feeding Hole

14¼"   5"

¼" Perch Hole   5"

BUILDING THE FEEDER

1 **Prepare the Feed Chamber Parts.** Cut the front, back, and sides to the dimensions in the Cutting List. Use a protractor or combination square to lay out the 45-degree roof angles on the front and back pieces. Make these cuts with a handsaw, saber saw, or circular saw. Drill three ¾-inch feeder holes in the front and back, and two similar holes in each side piece, as shown in Feed Chamber Layout. Drill the holes at a slight downward angle so the thistle won't spill as the seeds fall out from the screen. Drill ¼-inch holes for the perches 1-inch below the lip of each feeder hole.

Clamp the feed chamber front and back together, making sure all edges are flush, then drill a ⅜-inch dowel-keyhole through both pieces as shown in Feed Chamber Layout.

2 **Attach the Floor Cleats.** Cut the floor cleats to the dimensions in the Cutting List. Center the long cleats across the front and back and the short cleats across the sides, ½ inch from the bottom as shown in the Overall View. Attach the cleats with glue and brads.

3 **Assemble the Feed Chamber.** Cut two 2x12-inch pieces of wire mesh for the front and back sections and two 2x8-inch pieces for the side. Staple the pieces in place. Clip openings around the perch holes so the perches can poke through the screen.

Cut the 3x3-inch floor from ¼-inch plywood. Attach the two sides to the front and back pieces, with the floor in place, using glue and countersunk 1¼-inch screws on the sides and glue on the floor cleats. Insert wood plugs into the countersunk holes to conceal the screws. After the glue has dried, trim the plugs flush with a chisel and sand them smooth.

Overall View

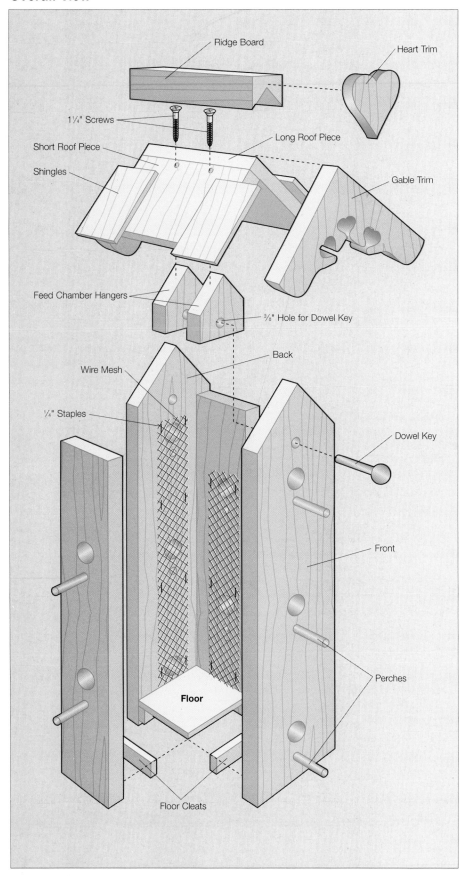

Ridge Board

Heart Trim

1¼" Screws

Short Roof Piece

Shingles

Long Roof Piece

Gable Trim

Feed Chamber Hangers

⅜" Hole for Dowel Key

Wire Mesh

Back

¼" Staples

Dowel Key

Front

Perches

Floor

Floor Cleats

5 Assemble the Roof and Feed Chamber Hangers.

Cut the long and short roof pieces to the dimensions in the Cutting List. Attach the long roof piece over the short one with glue and two 1¼-inch screws.

Cut the 3-inch-long feed chamber hangers from 1x3 scraps. Use a protractor or a combination square to lay out the 45-degree peak cuts at the top of the pieces. Clamp the pieces to a work surface, then make the peak cuts with a circular saw or handsaw.

Place the feed chamber hangers 2⅞ inches apart to fit inside the feed chamber. Center the roof over the hangers and fasten it with four countersunk 1¼-inch screws driven through the roof into the hangers. Use two screws for each hanger, positioning them as shown in the Overall View. Fill the holes with wood plugs.

6 Attach the Ridge Board.

Rip the ridge board from a piece of two-by stock to the dimensions in the Cutting List. Use a table saw to make the notch in the bottom of the board, as shown in Notching the Ridge Board. Set the saw-blade angle to 45 degrees, the length of cut to ⅞ inch, and the rip fence ⅛ inch from the blade as shown. On many table saws, the

Notching the Ridge Board

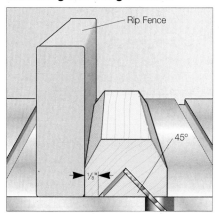

Rip Fence

45°

⅛"

blade tilts to the right from the operator's view. If you have such a saw, you'll have to put the rip fence to the left of the blade.

Using a push stick, run the piece through, flip it over, and run it through again to make the notch. As you near the end of the second cut, place a sacrificial piece of stock against the operator's end of the ridge board to prevent the triangular waste piece from shooting back at you when it's cut free. Attach the ridge board with two countersunk 1½-inch screws driven into the roof. Fill the holes with wood plugs.

7 Install the Dowel Key.

Position the roof assembly over the feeder. Using the dowel keyholes you already made in the front and back pieces as a guide, drill ⅜-inch holes through the feed-chamber hangers.

To make the dowel keys you'll have to drill into the wood balls and attach the dowels. Wood balls are available at most hobby stores and home centers. Clamp the balls in a vise between scraps of wood and drill ¼-inch holes ⅜ inch deep. If you don't have a vise, you can drill a ¾-inch hole in a scrap piece of wood, put a ball in the hole, and tape the ball in place. Then drill through the tape.

Cut two 2½-inch lengths from ¼-inch dowel material. Glue the wood dowels to the balls and place the dowels through the two keyholes to see that they hold correctly. Remove the "keys" and the roof assembly.

8 Attach the Trim. Reproduce

the Heart Trim Pattern and the Gable Trim Pattern on a photocopy machine set at 200 percent. If you don't have access to an enlarging photocopier, use the grids to make your own patterns. Clamp a couple of scraps of ⅜-inch plywood together and tape or glue the heart

Heart Trim Pattern

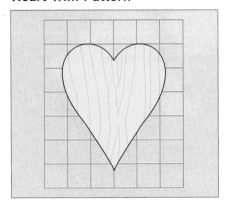

Gable Trim Pattern

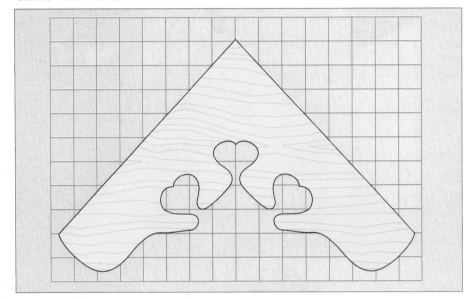

pattern on top. Cut out the two hearts together. Do the same for the gable trim. Make the cuts with a band saw, coping saw, or saber saw. On the gable trim, use a ⁷⁄₁₆-inch drill bit to create the tight curves in the upper heart shapes.

Cut the 1½x5-inch roof trim from ⅛-inch-thick hardboard. Attach the gable, heart, and roof trim to the roof with glue and brads.

9 Finish the Feeder. Cut

ten 2½-inch-long perches from ¼-inch wood dowels. Set the perches into their holes with glue. Paint the feeder, if you like, then put two screw eyes into the ridge board. If you don't paint the project, at least seal the edges of the plywood trim to prevent delamination. Attach wire or thin chain to the screw eyes and hang the feeder.

Gazebo Rest Stop

Its octagonal structure, fancy-cut railing, and sliced wood shingles and roof trim make the Gazebo Rest Stop a demanding—but at the same time satisfying—bird-feeder project to build.

T his project will take more time and effort than the other feeders in the book. But if you're prepared for—and capable of—the techniques involved, you'll build a bird feeder that looks spectacular.

Fancy fence pickets and rails give this octagon-shaped feeder a Victorian flair. The structure is large and can accommodate a number of birds. And you're not limited to putting food just in the feed chamber. There's plenty of room on the base to spread out a handful of berries and cut-up raisins to see whether you can attract some mockingbirds.

Unlike the other projects featured in this book, some advanced workshop equipment is mandatory to complete the feeder as shown. You'll need a band saw and a table saw, as well as a belt sander, web clamp, and router with roundover, chamfering, and rabbeting bits.

There's no doubt about it, though, the Gazebo Rest Stop is a first-class project. When you're done, you'll be able to place the feeder in your yard with pride.

CUTTING & MATERIALS LIST

Part	Quantity	Dimensions
Base Assembly		
Base	1	½"x17" octagon
Base trim	4	¾"x1½"x8"
Base trim	4	¾"x1½"x12½"
Post wrap	4	¾"x4"x17"
Feed Chamber Assembly		
Acrylic chamber sides	8	⅛"x1¾"x13"
Chamber bottom	1	¾"x5½"x5½"
Chamber legs	4	1"x1"x1½"
Pyramid disperser	1	2¼"x3½"x3½"
Side Assembly		
Sides	8	¾"x5¼"x12"
Roof-Deck Assembly		
Roof deck	8	½"x5½" (tapered to 2")x7"
Roof top	1	½"x5¼" octagon
Shingles	30	⅛"x2½"x9¼"
Roof trim	8	⅛"x1½"x10"
Cap Assembly		
Top	1	¾"x3" octagon
Forth tier	8	¼"x1"x1¼"

Part	Quantity	Dimensions
Third tier	1	¾"x5" octagon
Second tier	8	¼"x1⅜"x2⅝"
First tier	1	¾"x7" octagon
Insert	1	1½"x3" diameter
Bird	1	¾" thick, cut to shape
Wood dowel perch	1	¼" diameter x3"
Fence Assembly		
Top rails	8	⅜"x¾", cut to fit
Bottom rails	8	⅜"x¾", cut to fit
Fence posts	8	¾"x¾"x4"
Fence pickets	60	⅛" thick, cut to shape
Deck screws		1⅝" long
Deck screws		3" long
Brads		1" long
Brads		¾" long
Wood plugs		Sized to match the countersink
Silicone sealant		
Wood glue		
Plastic cement		

Difficulty Level: 🔨🔨🔨

BUILDING THE BASE AND FEED CHAMBER ASSEMBLY

1 Make the Base. Use a protractor and ruler or a combination square to lay out an octagon with 8-inch sides on a 17x17-inch piece of ½-inch plywood. Cut out the octagon. This will be the base.

Cut the base trim to the dimensions in the Cutting List and attach the boards to the base perimeter using countersunk 1⅝-inch screws and glue. The easiest way to attach the trim is to apply four boards, one to every other side of the octagon, then cut them flush with the line of the base meeting the board as shown in Applying Base Trim. Make the top of the trim flush with the top of the base. Add the other four boards and cut them flush with the outer edge of the adjacent trim boards. Fill the screw holes with wood plugs.

Next, make the post wrap, which will fit over a 4x4 post and support the feeder. Cut the pieces to the dimensions in the Cutting List. Enlarge the Post-Wrap Pattern using a photocopier set at 200 percent, cut out the paper pattern, and trace it onto rigid paperboard. Then cut the paperboard. If you can't get access to an enlarging photocopier, use the grid to make your own paperboard pattern. No matter how you make the patterns, don't cut out the notches yet. Use the paperboard pattern as a template to trace the shape onto

Applying Base Trim

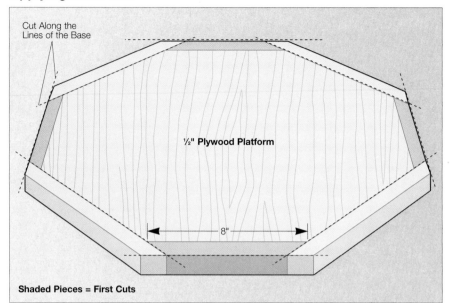

Cut Along the Lines of the Base

½" Plywood Platform

8"

Shaded Pieces = First Cuts

Post-Wrap Pattern

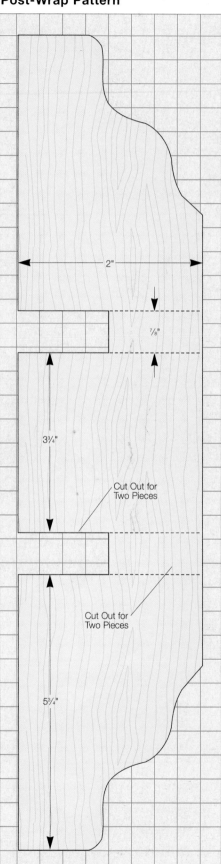

2"

⅞"

3¾"

Cut Out for Two Pieces

Cut Out for Two Pieces

5¾"

Post-Wrap Assembly

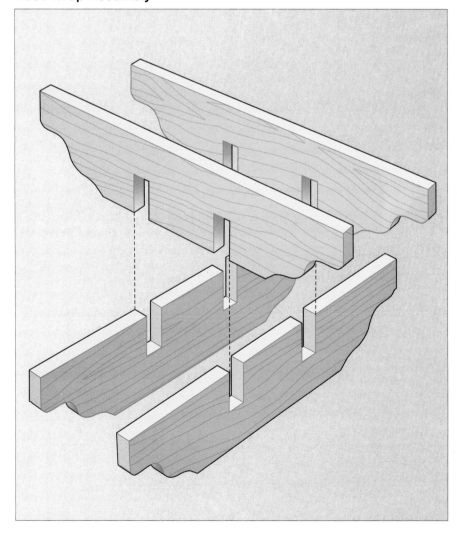

Overall View

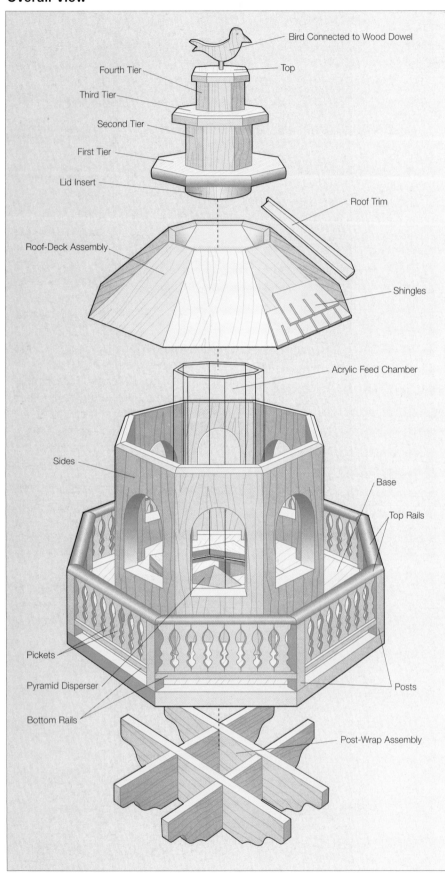

Bird Connected to Wood Dowel

Top

Fourth Tier

Third Tier

Second Tier

First Tier

Lid Insert

Roof Trim

Roof-Deck Assembly

Shingles

Acrylic Feed Chamber

Sides

Base

Top Rails

Pickets

Pyramid Disperser

Bottom Rails

Posts

Post-Wrap Assembly

the four precut pieces. Cut out the shapes with a band saw or saber saw.

Lay out the notches, following the dimensions shown in the Post-Wrap Pattern. Cut the sides of the notches with a handsaw or saber saw, then knock out the waste with a ³⁄₄-inch chisel cut across the bottom of each notch. Rout the bottom and side edges of the post-wrap sections with a roundover bit in a router or with a rasp and sandpaper. Interlock the pieces as shown, then center and attach the base using 1⁵⁄₈-inch screws and glue.

2 Construct the Feed Chamber Assembly. The feed chamber assembly consists of the plastic-panel feed chamber, chamber bottom, chamber legs, and pyramid disperser.

The feed chamber is made of eight pieces of acrylic glazing. Cut each piece of ¹⁄₈-inch acrylic 1³⁄₄ inches wide and 13 inches long. The long sides of the pieces should be miter-cut at a 22¹⁄₂-degree angle. Make these cuts using a band saw with a fine-tooth blade. Tilt the band-saw table for the angle cut.

Assemble the eight pieces forming the octagon-shaped feed chamber by holding them in place with several rubber bands. Next, take a tube of plastic cement and run the pointed spout along the inside and outside edges, allowing the chemical to bond the joints together. Set the chamber aside until the cement cures.

Cut the chamber bottom according to the dimensions in the Cutting List. Using the assembled feed chamber as a pattern, trace the outer edge of the shape onto the center of the chamber bottom. Mark a line ³⁄₈ inch inside the outline to serve as the cutting line. Drill a ¹⁄₄-inch starter hole and cut out the octagon shape with

Feed Chamber Assembly

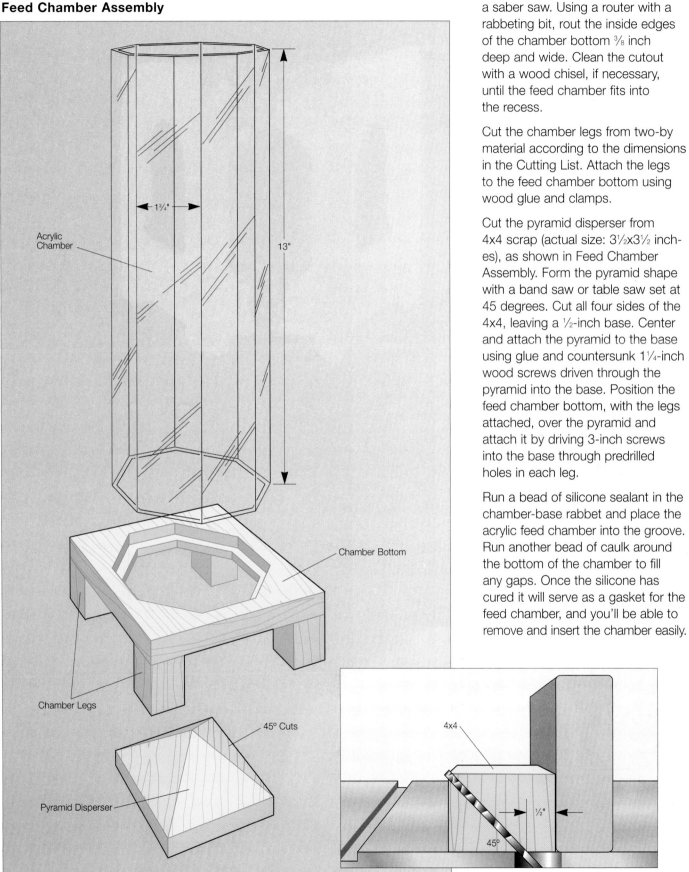

Acrylic
Chamber

1¾"

13"

Chamber Bottom

Chamber Legs

45° Cuts

Pyramid Disperser

4x4

½"

45°

a saber saw. Using a router with a rabbeting bit, rout the inside edges of the chamber bottom ⅜ inch deep and wide. Clean the cutout with a wood chisel, if necessary, until the feed chamber fits into the recess.

Cut the chamber legs from two-by material according to the dimensions in the Cutting List. Attach the legs to the feed chamber bottom using wood glue and clamps.

Cut the pyramid disperser from 4x4 scrap (actual size: 3½x3½ inches), as shown in Feed Chamber Assembly. Form the pyramid shape with a band saw or table saw set at 45 degrees. Cut all four sides of the 4x4, leaving a ½-inch base. Center and attach the pyramid to the base using glue and countersunk 1¼-inch wood screws driven through the pyramid into the base. Position the feed chamber bottom, with the legs attached, over the pyramid and attach it by driving 3-inch screws into the base through predrilled holes in each leg.

Run a bead of silicone sealant in the chamber-base rabbet and place the acrylic feed chamber into the groove. Run another bead of caulk around the bottom of the chamber to fill any gaps. Once the silicone has cured it will serve as a gasket for the feed chamber, and you'll be able to remove and insert the chamber easily.

BUILDING THE SIDE-PIECE AND ROOF ASSEMBLIES

1 Assemble the Octagon Sides. From a 1x6, cut the eight pieces that form the feeder's octagon sides. The side pieces must be miter-cut at a 22½-degree angle as shown in Gazebo Sides. Cut the central window openings and the openings at the bottom for the feed flow with a saber saw as shown in Gazebo Sides. Chamfer the top outside edge of each side piece as shown in the drawing using a router with a chamfering bit. Rout the outside edge of the window opening with a roundover bit.

Form the feeder's octagon shape with the eight side pieces standing upright on a flat surface. You'll need a web clamp to hold the pieces together. Apply wood glue to the sides of the gazebo pieces, then clamp them securely. Allow the assembly to dry thoroughly.

2 Make the Roof Deck. Use ½-inch plywood to make the roof deck. Each piece measures

Gazebo Sides

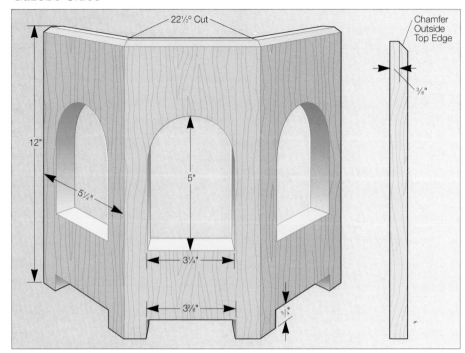

7 inches long by 5½ inches wide at the base and 2 inches wide at the crown. The long sides must be miter-cut at a 22½-degree angle. Cut the pieces, then chamfer the outside top edges with a router.

Gluing the roof pieces together can be difficult. The easiest way to do the job is to make a temporary support from a scrap piece of 4-inch-

diameter PVC pipe or similar-diameter cylindrical object like a drinking cup. You're going to end up with a structure that's approximately 4 inches tall, so the support should be at least 3½ inches tall. Assemble the roof pieces on a piece of plywood with the narrow ends on top of the support until you've put the roof octagon together as shown in Roof-Deck Assembly. You may have to adjust the height of the support with shims to make certain the pieces fit. Once you're satisfied with the test fit, glue the sides together with silicone sealant. To hold them in place, screw the bottom end of each piece into the work surface as shown in Roof-Deck Assembly. Put a flat piece of wood on the center and add some weight to push the pieces down and firmly together. Allow the assembly to dry thoroughly before proceeding.

3 Attach the Side-Piece and Roof Assemblies. Center the octagon side-piece assembly over the feed chamber assembly. Mark where the outer wall locations

Roof-Deck Assembly

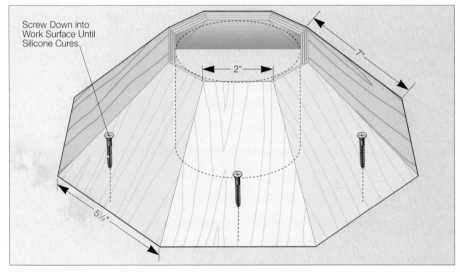

meet the base and drill holes into the base for 1⅝-inch screws to hold the side-piece assembly in place. Add wood glue to the bottom of the side-piece assembly where it will meet the base, set it in place, and screw it from underneath.

Place the roof assembly on top of the side-piece assembly. The roof will overlap the sides by about ¼ inch. Attach the roof to the top of the sides using glue and 1⅝-inch screws.

Using a belt sander, flatten the upper roof surface. Measure and cut a 5¼-inch octagon from ½-inch plywood, then cut a 3¼-inch circle in the center. Attach this piece to the top of the roof assembly using glue and 1-inch brads.

4 **Make the Cap Assembly.**
The cap assembly consists of the lid insert, first tier, second tier, third tier, fourth tier, and top, with wooden dowel and bird. The lid insert is a piece of 2x4 cut to a 3-inch diameter.

The second and fourth tiers are made of eight pieces each. Cut the tier pieces to the dimensions in the Cutting List with 22½-degree miters along the long edges. Cut the pieces and glue them together as shown in Cap Assembly.

The first tier, third tier, and top are cut from one-by lumber into octagon shapes 7 inches, 5 inches, and 3 inches in diameter, respectively. You can use 1x8s for all the octagons or use a 1x6 for the third tier and a 1x4 for the top. Use a protractor to lay out the angles for the first tier's 7-inch octagon, the third tier's 5-inch octagon, and the top's 3-inch octagon. Cut the pieces with a band saw or saber saw.

Rout the first tier and top using a roundover bit and a router pad to hold the pieces securely. Rout the third tier with a chamfering bit. Cen-

ter the insert under the first tier and attach it with a countersunk 2-inch screw. Next, center and glue the second tier, third tier, fourth tier, and top. Hold the assembly together with rubber bands or a web clamp until the glue cures.

Make the bird shown in Cap Assembly using the procedure described in Step 1 of "Building the Base and

Feed Chamber Assembly," page 92, except enlarge it twice, first to 200 percent, then to 150. Trace the bird onto one-by lumber and cut it out. Drill a ¼-inch-diameter hole about ¼ inch deep in the bottom of the bird and attach the wood dowel with glue. Now drill a ¼-inch hole in the top and attach the bird and dowel with glue.

Cap Assembly

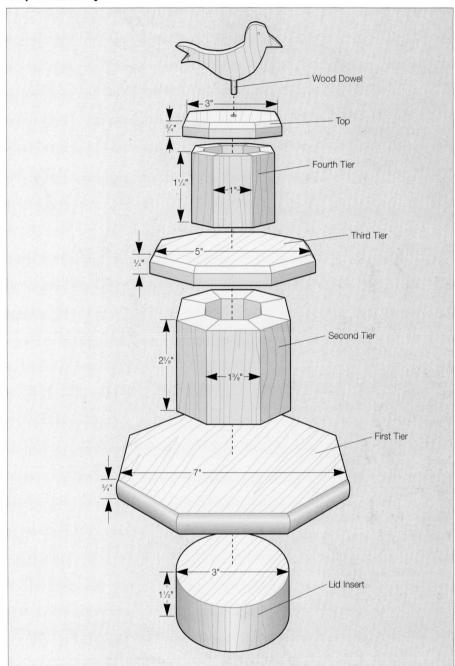

- Wood Dowel
- Top
- Fourth Tier
- Third Tier
- Second Tier
- First Tier
- Lid Insert

3"
¾"
1¼"
1"
5"
¾"
2⅝"
1⅜"
7"
¾"
3"
1½"

Fence Assembly

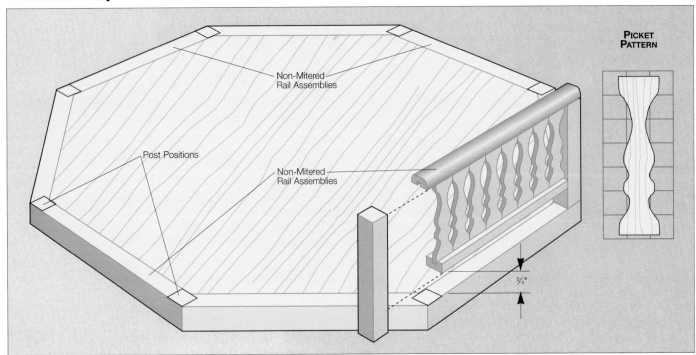

PICKET
PATTERN

Non-Mitered
Rail Assemblies

Post Positions

Non-Mitered
Rail Assemblies

³⁄₄"

Routing the Top Rail Edge

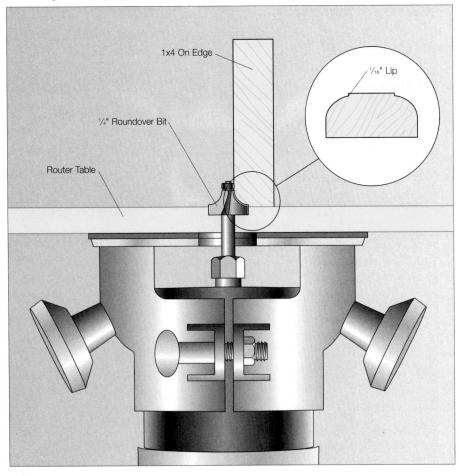

1x4 On Edge

¹⁄₁₆" Lip

¹⁄₄" Roundover Bit

Router Table

BUILDING THE FENCE

1 Cut the Fence Assembly.
The fence assembly consists of
the fence posts, the top and bottom
rails, and the pickets. First, cut the
eight fence posts from one-by material ³⁄₄x³⁄₄x4 inches.

For the railing, you'll need about
75 inches of top rail and about
66 inches of bottom rail. Using
1x4 stock, rout the two edges of
the top rail with a ¹⁄₄-inch round-
over bit set ¹⁄₁₆ inch deep as shown
in Routing the Top Rail Edge. Rip
the rail ³⁄₈ inch thick. Rip the 66-inch
bottom rail to the same ³⁄₈-inch thick-
ness but don't rout it. Cut ¹⁄₈-inch-
deep saw kerfs down the center
of each piece with a table saw as
shown in Cutting the Railing Groove.
Be sure to cut the kerf in the underside of the top rail.

Trace the fence picket shape from
Fence Assembly onto the narrow

Cutting the Railing Groove

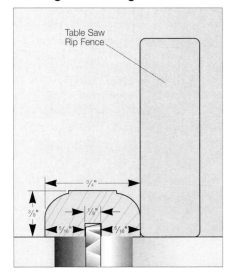

Shaping the Pickets

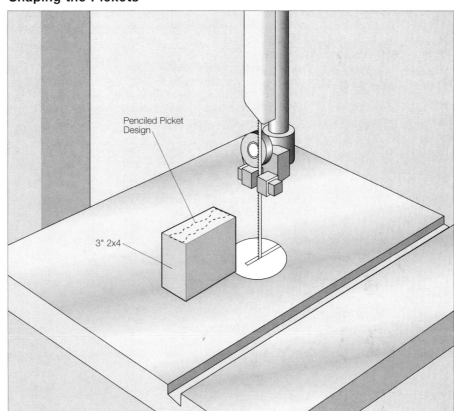

Slicing the Pickets

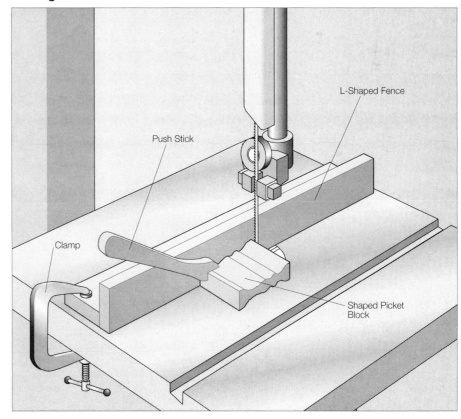

face of six 3-inch blocks of 2x4. You'll need a band saw with a narrow blade to cut the picket shape as shown in Shaping the Pickets. Next, make an L-shaped wood fence, leave a ⅛-inch space between the blade and the fence. Securely clamp the fence to the band-saw work surface. Bring the height adjustment to within 1½ inches of the surface as shown in Slicing the Pickets. Using a push stick, slice 60 decorative fence pickets.

2 **Build and Attach the Fence Assembly.** You'll have to make two kinds of fence assemblies, one with square cuts on the ends of the rails and the other with 45-degree mitered cuts. First, make four assemblies with square cuts. The assemblies will be attached to every other side of the octagon base as shown in Fence Assembly, and will hold seven pickets.

Fasten the eight fence posts cut earlier to the base, positioning them as shown in the drawing. Use 1⅝-inch screws driven up through the base and into the bottom of each post. Next, cut four top rails from the one long 75-inch piece that was made in Step 1. Cut each rail long enough to span the fence posts, outside to outside as shown in Fence Assembly. Measure carefully before cutting. Attach the top rail, kerf side down, to the posts with ¾-inch brads.

Cut the bottom rails to fit between the posts as shown in Fence Assembly. Run a bead of silicone in the top rails' saw kerfs and set the pickets. Now attach the bottom rails, with the saw kerfs facing upward, using silicone in the kerfs and 1-inch brads driven through the posts and into the rails.

Next, cut the remaining lengths of top and bottom rails 36 inches long each. Glue pickets into the saw kerfs, butting them together, to make one long assembly. Let the assembly dry, then cut sections with 45-degree mitered ends to fit between the assemblies already secured to the base. Glue the mitered assemblies to the ends of the posts with silicone. Use ¾-inch lifts made from scrap wood to hold the sections in place while the silicone sets up.

FINISHING THE FEEDER

1 Cut the Shingles and Roof Trim. Make the shingles by crosscutting eight 2½-inch-wide wood blocks from a 2x10 as shown in Cutting the Shingle Blocks. Cut kerfs on a band saw or table saw 1 inch deep and 1 inch apart along the length of each block as shown in Kerfing the Shingle Blocks. Using a table saw as shown in Slicing the Shingles or a band saw and the L-shaped fence mentioned in Step 1 of "Building the Fence," page 98, slice ⅛-inch-thick shingles using a push stick. You'll get about four shingle sections from each of the eight blocks.

Make the roof trim from a 10-inch length of 2x4. The process involves making multiple passes on a table saw as shown in Cutting the Ridge Trim. Rip the trim on a table saw with the blade tilted 12 degrees and set $^{13}/_{16}$ inch high. Adjust the fence to cut a ⅛-inch-thick piece of trim, with the larger portion of the 2x4 between the fence and the

Cutting the Shingle Blocks

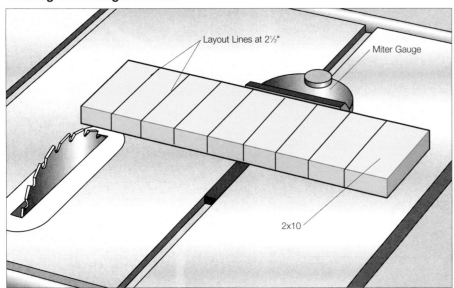

Layout Lines at 2½"

Miter Gauge

2x10

Kerfing the Shingle Blocks

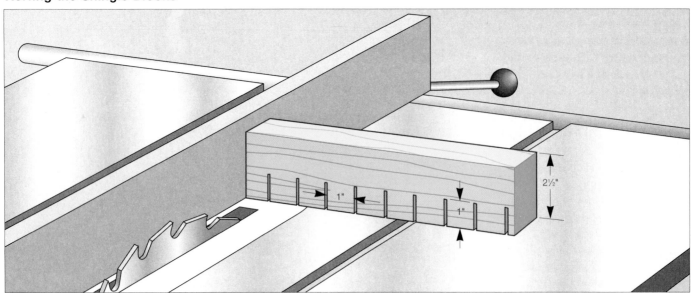

1"

1"

2½"

Slicing the Shingles

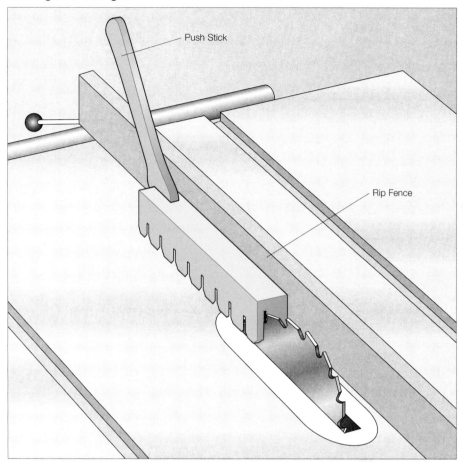

Push Stick

Rip Fence

Cutting the Ridge Trim

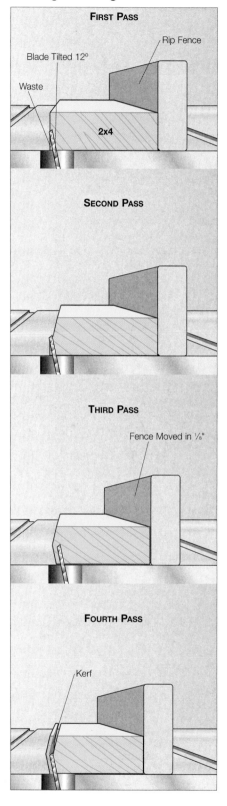

FIRST PASS

Rip Fence

Blade Tilted 12°

Waste

2x4

SECOND PASS

THIRD PASS

Fence Moved in ⅛"

FOURTH PASS

Kerf

blade, as in Cutting the Ridge Trim. Using a push stick, make the first pass. Reverse the board and make a second pass. Discard the waste. Adjust the fence again for a ⅛-inch cut, and make two passes to cut the first piece of trim. Keep adjusting the fence toward the blade ⅛ inch after each set of two passes to make the remaining seven trim pieces.

2 **Shingle the Roof.** Start the first course of shingles with an overlap of about 1 inch. Place the next row of shingles on top of the first with a 1-inch overlap, and so forth. Cut each succeeding length of shingles to fit the angle of the roof as it becomes narrower at the top. Secure the shingles with silicone sealant.

Attach the roof trim, allowing a ⅝-inch overhang from the shingles at the end of the roof. Let each piece of trim protrude slightly at the top, to be sanded later. Fasten the trim to the roof with silicone. When the silicone has dried, sand the trim flush with the plywood roof top.

3 **Making the Final Touches.** Seal the project with a water-repellent finish. Paint the feeder or stain it the color(s) of your choice. Place the feeder on top of a 4x4 post, and let all your neighbors envy your workmanship.

Glossary

American Goldfinch Best known for the canary yellow of the male in spring and summer, this small bird appears throughout the United States and is especially fond of thistle seed.

Baffle An obstacle purposely placed around a bird feeder to keep out unwanted competitors and predators.

Band Saw A saw with a blade made from a steel loop driven by two wheels inside a casing to provide a continuous cutting edge for making curved cuts.

Brad A finishing nail smaller than 1 inch.

Butt Joint A joint where one piece of wood is simply butted against the other.

Chickadee A common backyard bird that ranges across much of the United States, except the extreme south. Its common characteristics are a black cap and throat, white cheeks, a gray back, and light underparts.

Chromated Copper Arsenic (CCA) A chemical used to treat lumber under high pressure so the wood can resist decay.

Circular Saw A hand-held power saw consisting of a circular disk, usually with a toothed edge.

Competitors Animals that want to eat the birds' food.

Coping Saw A saw with a thin, narrow blade held in a frame and used to make curved cuts. The blade can also be conveniently detached and reattached through the starter hole of an inside cut.

Crest The pointed tuft of feathers found on the heads of some birds.

Crosscut A cut that is made across the grain on a piece of wood.

Decay The destruction of wood by bacteria, fungi, and the like.

Depth Stop On a drill, a collar that stops the bit when it reaches a desired depth.

Downy Woodpecker A black-and-white sparrow-sized bird with a pointed beak; the male Downy has a large red spot on the back of the neck. Downies range throughout the United States, except the extreme Southwest.

Eaves Lower edge of a sloped roof that projects over the outside wall.

Gable The triangular area of a structure made by the sloping ends of a ridged roof.

Grain The direction and arrangement of wood fibers in a piece of wood.

Hardwood Wood that comes from deciduous trees, or those that lose their leaves in fall.

Jig A device for holding a workpiece, or attached to a workpiece, that allows a tool to cut the piece safely and accurately.

Kerf The space created by a saw blade as it cuts through wood.

Kickback The dangerous action that happens when a saw suddenly jumps backward out of a cut, or when a stationary power saw throws a piece of wood back at the operator.

Knot The high-density root of limbs that is not connected to the surrounding wood.

Lumber Grade A label that reflects the lumber's natural growth characteristics or defects that result from milling errors and manufacturing techniques.

Miter Joint A joint in which the ends of two boards are cut at equal angles (typically 45 degrees) to form a corner.

Nail Set A pointed tool with one round or square end, used to drive nails flush with or below the surface of wood.

Northern Cardinal A bird commonly found in the eastern United States. The male is brilliant red with a head crest and black face mask; the female is reddish brown with a bright red beak.

Penny (abbr. d) Unit of measurement for nail length; e.g., a 10d nail is 3 inches long.

Plywood Veneers of wood glued together in a sandwich. Each veneer is oriented perpendicular to the next.

Predators Animals that want to eat the birds at bird feeders.

Pressure-Treated Lumber Wood that has had preservatives, specifically CCA, forced into it under pressure so it can repel rot and insects.

Rake The part of the roof that projects over the gable ends.

Redwood A straight-grain weather-resistant wood used for outdoor building.

Ridge The horizontal line at which two roof planes meet and down from which both roof planes slope.

Rip Cut A cut made with the grain on a piece of wood.

Router A power tool that is shaped like a canister and has a bit protruding from the bottom for finishing edges and making grooves, dadoes, and rabbets.

Saber Saw Also known as a jigsaw. A portable electric saw with a straight blade that cuts in an up and down motion.

Scroll Saw A stationary or bench-top power saw with a thin reciprocating blade used to cut even, tight curves.

Softwood Wood, such as cedar, cypress, fir, hemlock, pine, redwood, and spruce, that comes from coniferous trees. Some kinds of softwood are used outdoors because they are naturally rot resistant.

Suet A high-energy bird food commonly made from the trimmed, hard fat of kidneys and loins of beef or lamb. Suet can also be rendered from animal fat and mixed with peanut butter and seeds.

Table Saw A stationary power saw that can be used for crosscutting, ripping, grooving, and dadoing lumber. It can also be used for some kinds of joinery.

Tufted Titmouse A gray bird with biege-and-rust-colored underparts, the titmouse's predominant feature is a crest it shows when feeling aggressive. It ranges throughout the eastern United States.

Waste Cut The part of the cut that can be used for scrap or thrown away.

Index

Adhesives for bird feeders, 11, 13
Apples, 8, 19, 31

Baffles, 8, 9
Bird Feeder/Robin's Roost, 33, 63-67
    building instructions for, 65-67
    cutting and materials list for, 64
Bird feeders
    construction of, 11, 13
        adhesives in, 11, 13
        fasteners in, 11
        finishes in, 13
        tools in, 12
        wood in, 11
    hanger for, 22-23
    placement of, 7
Bird-Feedosaurus, 31-32, 36
    building instructions for, 32
    cutting and materials list for, 31
Bird foods, 8, 10, 13
Birds
    making commitment to feeding, 13
    needs of, 7
    reasons for feeding, 7
Birdseed, 8, 10
    Bird Feeder/Robin's Roost for, 33, 63-67
    Chickadee Feeder for, 38, 48-50
    Feline Feeding Stand for, 37, 54-57
    Gazebo Rest Stop for, 33, 91-101
    Milk-Jug Seed Depot for, 37, 46-47
    Multilevel Seed Silo for, 36, 71-73
    Pig Bird Feeder for, 35, 82-86
    Seed and Suet Storehouse for, 40, 58-62
    Seed Bell Shelter for, 36, 78-81
    Seed, Suet, and Water Station for, 39,
        41-45
    Swiss Chalet for, 14-18, 34
    Thistle Seed Dispenser for, 39, 87-90
    Tin-Can Seed Shoppe for, 35, 68-70
Blackbirds
    Multilevel Seed Silo for, 71
    Swiss Chalet for, 14
Bluebirds, Bird-Feedosaurus for, 31
Blue Jays, Hanging Apples for, 19-23, 37
Bread scraps, 8
Bulk foods
    Bird-Feedosaurus for, 31-32, 36
    Cozy Cottage for, 38, 51-53
    Hanging Apples for, 19

Cardinals
    Hanging Apples for, 19
    Multilevel Seed Silo for, 71
    Northern Cardinal, 6
    Tin-Can Seed Shoppe for, 68
Chickadee Feeder, 38, 48-50
    building instructions for, 49-50
    cutting and materials list for, 49

Chickadees, 6, 8
    Chickadee Feeder for, 38, 48-50
    Hanging Apples for, 19-23, 37
    Thistle Seed Dispenser for, 39, 87-90
Competitors, discouraging, 7-8
Corn
    Cracked, 8, 71
    On-the-cob, 74
Cozy Cottage, 38, 51-53
    building instructions for, 52-53
    cutting and materials list for, 52

Doves
    Hanging Apples for, 19
    Multilevel Seed Silo for, 71

Fasteners for bird feeders, 11
Feline Feeding Stand, 37, 54-57
    building instructions for, 55-57
    cutting and materials list for, 55
Finishes for bird feeders, 13
Flicker, Swiss Chalet for, 14

Gazebo Rest Stop, 33, 91-101
    building instructions for, 92-101
    cutting and materials list for, 92
Goldfinches
    American Goldfinch, 13
    Thistle Seed Dispenser for, 87
    Tin-Can Seed Shoppe for, 68

Hanging Apples, 19-23, 37
    building instructions for, 20-21
    cutting and materials list for, 20

Juncos, Multilevel Seed Silo for, 71

Log, daily or weekly, 10

Metric conversion charts, 104
Milk-Jug Seed Depot, 37, 46-47
    building instructions for, 47
    cutting and materials list for, 46
Mockingbirds
    Bird-Feedosaurus for, 31
    Gazebo Rest Stop for, 91
Multilevel Seed Silo, 36, 71-73
    building instructions for, 72-73
    cutting and materials list for, 72

Nuts, 8

Orioles, Bird-Feedosaurus for, 31

Paint, 13
Pig Bird Feeder, 35, 82-86
    building instructions for, 84-86
    cutting and materials list for, 83
Pine Siskin, Thistle Seed Dispenser for, 87
Predators, discouraging, 7-8

Robins
    Bird Feeder/Robin's Roost for, 63
    Bird-Feedosaurus for, 31

Safety tips, 3
Seed and Suet Storehouse, 40, 58-62
    building instructions for, 59-62
    cutting and materials list for, 59
Seed Bell Shelter, 36, 78-81
    building instructions for, 80-81
    cutting and materials list for, 79
Seed, Suet, and Water Station, 39, 41-45
    building instructions for, 42-45
    cutting and materials list for, 42
Sparrows
    Bird-Feedosaurus for, 31
    Hanging Apples for, 19
    Multilevel Seed Silo for, 71
Squirrel Feeder, 8, 34, 74-77
    building instructions for, 75-77
    cutting and materials list for, 75
Starlings, 8
    Hanging Apples for, 19
Suet, 8, 10, 24
    Seed and Suet Storehouse for, 58
    Seed, Suet, and Water Station for, 41
    Suet Holder for, 24
Suet Holder, 24-27, 40
    building instructions for, 25-27
    cutting and materials list for, 25
Sunflower seeds, 8, 74
Swiss Chalet, 14-18, 34
    building instructions for, 15-18
    cutting and materials list for, 15

Thistle Seed Dispenser, 39, 87-90
    building instructions for, 88-90
    cutting and materials list for, 88
Tin-Can Seed Shoppe, 35, 68-70
    building instructions for, 70-73
    cutting and materials list for, 69
Titmice
    Tin-Can Seed Shoppe for, 35, 68-70
    Tufted Titmouse, 13
Tools for bird feeders, 12

Water
    bird needs for, 7, 8, 11
    Seed, Suet, and Water Station for, 41-45
    Watering Hole for, 28
Watering Hole, 28-30, 38
    building instructions for, 29-30
    cutting and materials list for, 28
Wild bird food mixes, 8
Wood choices for bird feeders, 11
Woodpeckers, Downy, 8
Wood sealer/preservative, 13

Metric Conversion Charts

LUMBER

Sizes: Metric cross sections are so close to their nearest U.S. sizes, as noted at right, that for most purposes they may be considered equivalents.

Lengths: Metric lengths are based on a 300mm module, which is slightly shorter in length than an U.S. foot. It will, therefore, be important to check your requirements accurately to the nearest inch and consult the table below to find the metric length required.

Areas: The metric area is a square meter. Use the following conversion factor when converting from U.S. data: *100 sq. feet = 9.29 sq. meters.*

METRIC LENGTHS

Lengths Meters	Equivalent Feet and Inches
1.8m	5' 10⅞"
2.1m	6' 10⅝"
2.4m	7' 10½"
2.7m	8' 10¼"
3.0m	9' 10⅛"
3.3m	10' 9⅞"
3.6m	11' 9¾"
3.9m	12' 9½"
4.2m	13' 9⅜"
4.5m	14' 9⅓"
4.8m	15' 9"
5.1m	16' 8¾"
5.4m	17' 8⅝"
5.7m	18' 8⅜"
6.0m	19' 8¼"
6.3m	20' 8"
6.6m	21' 7⅞"
6.9m	22' 7⅝"
7.2m	23' 7½"
7.5m	24' 7¼"
7.8m	25' 7⅛"

Dimensions are based on 1m = 3.28 feet, or 1 foot = 0.3048m

METRIC SIZES (SHOWN BEFORE NEAREST U.S. EQUIVALENT)

Millimeters	Inches	Millimeters	Inches
16 x 75	⅝ x 3	44 x 150	1¾ x 6
16 x 100	⅝ x 4	44 x 175	1¾ x 7
16 x 125	⅝ x 5	44 x 200	1¾ x 8
16 x 150	⅝ x 6	44 x 225	1¾ x 9
19 x 75	¾ x 3	44 x 250	1¾ x 10
19 x 100	¾ x 4	44 x 300	1¾ x 12
19 x 125	¾ x 5	50 x 75	2 x 3
19 x 150	¾ x 6	50 x 100	2 x 4
22 x 75	⅞ x 3	50 x 125	2 x 5
22 x 100	⅞ x 4	50 x 150	2 x 6
22 x 125	⅞ x 5	50 x 175	2 x 7
22 x 150	⅞ x 6	50 x 200	2 x 8
25 x 75	1 x 3	50 x 225	2 x 9
25 x 100	1 x 4	50 x 250	2 x 10
25 x 125	1 x 5	50 x 300	2 x 12
25 x 150	1 x 6	63 x 100	2½ x 4
25 x 175	1 x 7	63 x 125	2½ x 5
25 x 200	1 x 8	63 x 150	2½ x 6
25 x 225	1 x 9	63 x 175	2½ x 7
25 x 250	1 x 10	63 x 200	2½ x 8
25 x 300	1 x 12	63 x 225	2½ x 9
32 x 75	1¼ x 3	75 x 100	3 x 4
32 x 100	1¼ x 4	75 x 125	3 x 5
32 x 125	1¼ x 5	75 x 150	3 x 6
32 x 150	1¼ x 6	75 x 175	3 x 7
32 x 175	1¼ x 7	75 x 200	3 x 8
32 x 200	1¼ x 8	75 x 225	3 x 9
32 x 225	1¼ x 9	75 x 250	3 x 10
32 x 250	1¼ x 10	75 x 300	3 x 12
32 x 300	1¼ x 12	100 x 100	4 x 4
38 x 75	1½ x 3	100 x 150	4 x 6
38 x 100	1½ x 4	100 x 200	4 x 8
38 x 125	1½ x 5	100 x 250	4 x 10
38 x 150	1½ x 6	100 x 300	4 x 12
38 x 175	1½ x 7	150 x 150	6 x 6
38 x 200	1½ x 8	150 x 200	6 x 8
38 x 225	1½ x 9	150 x 300	6 x 12
44 x 75	1¾ x 3	200 x 200	8 x 8
44 x 100	1¾ x 4	250 x 250	10 x 10
44 x 125	1¾ x 5	300 x 300	12 x 12

Dimensions are based on 1 inch = 25mm